BEYOND THE INVESTOR'S QUOTIENT

The Inner World of Investing

Jacob Bernstein

JOHN WILEY & SONS

New York   Chichester   Brisbane   Toronto   Singapore

Library of Congress Cataloging in Publication Data:

Bernstein, Jacob, 1946–
    Beyond the investor's quotient.

    Bibliography: p.
    Includes index.
    1. Investments. 2. Investments—Psychological
aspects. I. Title.

HG4521.B443 1985   332.6   85-12325
ISBN 0-471-82062-8

Printed in the United States of America

10   9   8   7   6   5   4   3   2   1

Preface

In 1980 I wrote *The Investor's Quotient*, a book that sought to bring the importance of investor and trader psychology into the active perception of all who seek to multiply their money. Since publication, *The Investor's Quotient* has not only been read and studied by thousands of investors throughout the world, but it has also prompted wide acclaim from the media and the investing public. Rarely a day passes that I fail to receive either a letter or telephone call from an individual who has read the book and who now feels the need for more information. Although it is generally believed that trading systems are more important than traders, I know, for a fact, that traders are clearly and unequivocally more important than systems. A system without a trader is like a computer without a programmer or a spacecraft without a pilot. A complex piece of machinery which costs millions to develop must, after all is said and done, be guided, piloted, directed, and tested by a human being. Awareness of this fact is slowly but surely reaching the investing public. It is, however, a difficult fact for most people to acknowledge. The symptoms of need are, nevertheless, brought to my attention almost daily.

The thirst for more information is merely one aspect of increased investor awareness. How many losses does it take before a trader becomes aware of the fact that something is dreadfully wrong? How many new and glorious, "ultimate, perfect, foolproof, fail-safe" systems must the trader use before he or she begins to realize that virtually any system that is systematic will do what's necessary in the way of generating profits? The calls and letters I've been receiving since 1980 come from progressive investors who have embarked on an exciting journey of self-discovery, not only in their lives as traders and investors, but in their personal lives and interpersonal relationships as well. They realize that the search for profits is inseparable from the search for self. In making these claims, it is not my intent to place profitability and metaphysical advancement on the same plane. I make the comparison merely to reinforce the fact that self-awareness and the evolution of higher level personal awareness are the building blocks of success in trading and investing. Indeed, metaphysical and spiritual growth are ultimately necessary for most other forms of growth. Paradoxically, however, highly evolved philosophical and spiritual growth may lead to the rejection of financial motivation.

My purpose in writing this book is threefold: First, I want to improve the lot of the investor. As strange as this might sound to you, I want to bring traders and investors out of the dark ages of systems trading. Why strange? Because we have been led, falsely, I believe, to assume that computerization and its natural outgrowth, systematization, are the investor's messiahs. This, as I will show later on, is perhaps the most dangerous myth ever to be accepted by the investing public. It is my goal to help undo what has unwittingly been done by the "age of computer hype."

As the future of the free-world economies has become more tenuous, and more responsive to political events, investors have found themselves more and more at the mercy of their emotions. Therefore, my second reason for writing this book has been to provide investors and speculators with viable tools for coping with the present state of the investment and speculative worlds.

My third reason for writing this book was to express insights and experiences which have changed my perceptions since the publication of *The Investor's Quotient*. We all grow in response to our experiences. The process is called "learning." In my position as trader, advisor, newsletter writer, and author, I am exposed daily to situations which shape my learning at a rate which is, perhaps, more accelerated than the norm. By dealing with many problems, both my own and those of others, I have had experiences and learned solutions which may take other people a longer time to learn. Do I have all the answers? By no means! However, I have had understandings and insights which might prove very helpful to those who have not been exposed to the same situations and experiences that I have.

My greatest task in writing this book was to produce a quality product which was not a redundancy of *The Investor's Quotient*. In fact, what I sought to achieve was a book that picked up where *The Investor's Quotient* left off. Admittedly, my first efforts were merely to rewrite *The Investor's Quotient* in a more thorough fashion which would, perhaps, make the book easier to understand. In fact, I hired a writer, Barbara Glatt, with the instructions that *The Investor's Quotient* be outlined, detailed, and expanded. Barbara did a wonderful job with the *IQ* book and her efforts are appreciated. Yet, in spite of the time and money I spent in having Barbara do the job, I felt that I needed to produce something that was more than a rewrite of what I had published before. I decided that it was necessary to examine some new issues and to provide some pragmatic techniques for dealing with them on the level of behavioral change.

Therefore, I began this book "from scratch," seeking to achieve these goals. Unfortunately I did not get to incorporate anything but the most basic concepts from *The Investor's Quotient*. I am satisfied that I have achieved my goal of producing a work that would be unique, instructive, specific, and one which, above all, could stand on its own.

It has often been said that success in anything can only come as the result of hard work. However, hard work in the wrong direction can rarely lead to success. In the markets it is not only important to work hard, but it is perhaps more important to work toward proper goals. *The Investor's Quotient* defined the existence of a problem and offered some solutions and goals. This book seeks to help you work hard with a greater understanding of goals. This book will help you refine your direction, define objectives, select methods of attaining goals, and determine ways by which the road to success can remain visible. This book will not provide answers which are necessarily simple to put into practice, nor will it mislead you into thinking that success is a matter of overnight change.

It is my most sincere wish that all who read this book will benefit. Benefit is potential energy which expresses itself as the kinetic energy of positive change. In the intricate universe of the human mind, small changes can set large changes into motion. It takes only a small snowslide to produce an immense avalanche. It takes only a simple idea to stimulate complex technological achievement. If, therefore, only one or two of my simple ideas can effect change in only a few readers, then the results could easily grow into an avalanche of positive results. Perhaps I am a wishful thinker, a daydreamer, an idealist . . . I hope my expectations are not unrealistic. I will know only by your feedback.

JACOB BERNSTEIN

Winnetka, Illinois
December 1985

Acknowledgments

My thanks are extended to all who helped make this book possible. Far too numerous to mention, I include in this acknowledgment the many people who have written and called me with questions, thanks, comments, and suggestions. I thank my family, my staff, my colleagues, my publishing company, my editor, my peers, and fellow traders. I have grown from every experience, positive, negative, or neutral.

J. B.

Contents

1

Why This Book
Was Written and
What It Can
Do for You

The 1970s and 1980s have been witness to a growing movement toward self-awareness, self-actualization, and self-discovery. The movement has not only been evident in the so-called free world, but there have also been rumblings from behind the Iron Curtain and China. Cyclic forces are most likely the cause of this trend toward metaphysical and spiritual growth, and these cyclic forces are closely related to the long wave economic cycles which were, paradoxically, theorized and studied by the Soviet economist N. D. Kondratieff in the early 1900s. Certainly, the roots of such movements date back to Greco-Roman times. It is the nature of civilizations to place materialistic growth well ahead of spiritual growth and, alas, the existential and metaphysical growth phase of civilizations often marks the peak in their evolutionary process. It is most certainly a sad irony, yet the same cycle has been played out countless times.

The same metamorphosis can be observed in the investor,

trader, or speculator. I lump all three together since they are essentially cut from the same fabric with varying degrees of objectives and time frames in the marketplace. The first goal of most investors is to "strike it rich," to "make it big," to "make a killing," or to "beat the market." Investors often think that they are like the ancient world explorers or the American pioneers for whom there was a sense of danger, of the unknown, and the promise of fabulous reward for their efforts. Heroes set out to conquer the American West or to discover lucrative trade routes to the Orient. There was intrigue, heroism, cowardice, romance, cunning, secrecy, planning, study, intense emotion, and thievery in the "old times." These same values, emotions, and attitudes form the subliminal base of what attracts many investors to the marketplace. Since the motives, fantasies, and expectations are not within the conscious awareness of the players, there is no need for guilt, no need for shame, and, sadly, very often no need to be in touch with investment realities.

The typical investor places goals ahead of means. When perceived goals are exceptionally desirable, there is frequently a tendency to ignore realities. This is why, for example, hundreds of people will wait long hours in a line in order to purchase lottery tickets. This is why young people will camp overnight at ticket counters, often outdoors in terrible weather, in order to purchase tickets to see their rock heroes or idols. Evidently, the perceived goal is worth the considerable effort, cost, suffering and discomfort. Similarly, many investors will go through "fire and water" to perfect elaborate trading systems. They will purchase countless newsletter services, personal consultations from leading experts, and complex computer systems in efforts to achieve the ultimate goal of market victory.

In sharp contrast to individuals who seek success without sufficient attention to process, those who have indeed achieved success frequently attribute their victory to the right combination of attitude, motivation, common sense, and good fortune. Somewhere in this combination is a method, a technique, a system, a means to an end. This does not mean that system alone is useless. There are and will be many individuals who attain success without any sense of personal development, philosophical growth, or personal awareness. When such things happen, however, they are often, upon close examination, attributable to good fortune, "A Sixth Sense," family circumstance, cunning, compromise, or even some illegalities. After all is said and done, many of these individuals either lose what they achieved or find self-awareness through "the back door."

Given the immense growth of the self-awareness movement, it is indeed strange that its roots have left the area of investor psychology virtually untouched. Prior to the publication of *The Investor's Quotient* (1980) there was only a handful of books available on the topic of investor psychology. It was left to the motivated individual to seek out the writings of the investment masters and to glean from these works whatever valuable morsels he or she could in regard to emotional attitudes and psychological factors in the areas of stock and futures trading. One of the classics in this respect still remains the purported life story of Jesse Livermore, written by Edwin LeFevre and entitled *Reminiscences of a Stock Operator*. Today, there is still a dearth of solid material available to those who seek to improve their investment psychology.

When I wrote *The Investor's Quotient*, I had numerous goals but they were primarily directed toward educating the investing public in the behaviors, attitudes, and emotions that create winners.

I quote from the Introduction:

> "Investigate before you invest," we are told. "Know corporate management, earnings reports, long-term debt, and projected sales," we are cautioned. The emphasis is, and has long been, on *market knowledge*. Yet, despite the voluminous output of market information, financial reports, advisory publications, and brokerage-house material, there are still many individuals who fail to profit from their investments. In fact, an overwhelming majority of public investors are net losers, year in, year out.

> Some speculative markets such as commodity futures are well-known for their ability to relieve traders of their funds in relatively short order. And yet, there are those who have managed to profit handsomely from their speculative and investment ventures in the marketplace. Paradoxically, our computerized technology and lightning-fast communications may have actually inhibited investment success. With our economic forecasting ability as well developed as it has become, market winners should be in the overwhelming majority. But they are not. The question naturally arises as to why. To one who is familiar with the basics of human psychology,

the answer is quite simple. However, remediating the underlying problem is complex. For it is the individual who stands in his or her own way.

For reasons, unknown to most, the emotional workings of each individual can be the determining factor in trading success or failure. This has long been common knowledge among successful investors.

The time has come to rekindle knowledge of the self and how it relates to the marketplace. It is now necessary to return to the most basic of basics— the human mind. It is to this end that I will strive.

Today, my motives are essentially similar to those I had in 1980. However, there are some substantive changes which have been inspired by the passage of time, by my own growth, by public response to *The Investor's Quotient*, but moreover, by my discussions with those who have demonstrated a keen interest in self-improvement.

The goals of this book are therefore threefold:

1. To provide a detailed explanation of the emotional, attitudinal, perceptual, and stimulus–response factors which form the basis of investor behavior and which can work either to the success or failure of the investor.
2. To provide methods and evaluative techniques by which self-awareness of such factors may be improved and, in so doing, initiate the process of change.
3. To provide tools for self-improvement; tools that are specific, effective, and pragmatic. While it is not expected that this book will provide answers to all who seek assistance, I do believe that it will help one get started in the right direction, a direction which should be illuminated by the light of increased profits.

ORGANIZATION AND STRUCTURE

This book discusses four basic categories of investor behavior:

1. *Understanding Investor Psychology.* This area outlines the basics of investor psychology, highlights the key elements of

investor psychology, and traces the origin and development of trading behavior.

2. *Self-Evaluation—Where Do You Fit?* This area provides a variety of methods and procedures by which the investor/trader can analyze his or her motivation, market attitudes, and psychological trading preparedness.

3. *Instituting Change.* This area discusses how to change what you don't like and how to eliminate unwanted behaviors replacing them with profitable trading behaviors. Various methods and procedures for facilitating progress are proposed.

4. *Continuing the Growth Process.* This area will teach you how to continue the growth process, how to avoid the pitfalls of emotional response to the marketplace, and how to improve your trading and investing during times of crisis, personal difficulty, and "choppy" markets. This area also provides a concise reading list.

IN ORDER TO GET THE MOST OUT OF THIS BOOK

Some books are written merely to read. Other books are written to be studied. This book is intended to be lived. I can tell you, from vast personal experiences with the markets since 1967, that the single best way to improve your profitability and relationship with the marketplace is not merely to study and understand new concepts, but also to experience them in as direct a way as possible. I've often heard it said that investors should "paper trade" markets in order to obtain a good sense of what to expect, how they will react, and the pitfalls they may encounter. I have also heard it said that nothing can replace experience. I am a realist. I place great value on "real time," experiencing, and coping with reality since, in the long run, reality is all we have. To experience reality does not mean that one must eliminate fantasy. It merely means that every aspect of human experience has its appropriate place. I maintain that "paper trading" is not reality. In fact, I believe that it can do more harm than good and that such trading or practice trading be *limited to only one or two brief exercises.* How can paper trading possibly hurt? What could be harmful about creating an unreal trading situation? The greatest danger rests in self-deception. Paper trading imposes no pressures. It does not place any real strain on the individual. Therefore, decisions are not subject to the intense emotional forces always hard at work in the marketplace. Decisions made in a paper trade situation will, most often, be good ones. However, when the same individual is placed in a real situation, the results are often drastically different. The comparison is akin to what I call the "educated fool" (one of the personality types discussed in Chapter 5).

The "educated fool" is an individual who has collected considerable education in his or her lifetime. Frequently this individual has several degrees from prestigious colleges and universities. He or she has often had works published in scholarly books and magazines and may even have written several texts. The educated fool's book knowledge is immense and often intimidating to others. But when it comes to pragmatics, to changing a light bulb, to making a simple auto repair, to doing garden work, this individual is totally inept. We have all known people like this. They are wonderful theoreticians and are extremely good at dealing with complex concepts but almost totally helpless in the practical application of their concepts and skills. There are additional traits to be discussed later. My point here is that to avoid being an educated fool, you must put the suggestions and concepts of this book into action. Action is the key word. Action will give you feedback. It will teach you a physical response by its consequences. It will teach you what actually works in the real world, and it will provide you with the positive feedback you need in order to continue the learning process. Action teaches better than anything I know.

Therefore, in order for you to get the most out of this book, I have a number of specific suggestions, all to be taken seriously.

1. Study the organization and chapter headings so that you may see what is in store for you.
2. Make an outline of the book as you progress.

3. Place key words and phrases on index cards and have them at your disposal for quick reference.

4. Be honest with yourself in answering questions in the evaluation sections.

5. When you feel that a given concept or statement makes good sense to you or when you can see that what has been said has merit, attempt to put it into practice immediately.

6. Do not attempt to master everything at once. The process may take several months to a year. You can, however, expect to see rather quick results but only on a small scale.

7. Set aside a given time of the day or week for this book. This time should be one which is relatively free from interruption and pressure.

8. When I ask you to engage in a given exercise, please do so. Don't merely pretend you are doing so. Remember that *experience* is important and that without experience, insight is nothing more than romanticism.

9. If you are not pleased with your trading results at the present time, then have the courage to either slow down your trading or completely stop until you have internalized some of the ideas in this book.

10. Recruit help from those around you where I have so indicated. Don't be afraid to ask for help, and don't be afraid to ask questions.

11. Attempt to isolate yourself from the "news" for a while. News in the marketplace is important; however, it may be destructive to your particular style of trading. Set the news on the back burner for a while and allow my news to enter your mind.

12. Attempt to understand your personal life in terms of the concepts I've proposed and outlined. Much of what I've said, perhaps all of it, is directly related to real life interpersonal relationships. Remember that success in the markets cannot be entirely separated from success in your personal life. One affects the other in a complex interplay. I don't

believe that you can change one area of your life without significantly affecting others.

13. When you feel the need for more reading or understanding in a given area, seek out the information. Chances are that this particular area is an important one for you and that you really do need more information. So go and get it.

14. The answers are not the same for everyone. We are all different. We have all had different experiences and different backgrounds. Therefore, what is a problem to one trader may not be a problem to another. Some chapters and concepts will be more meaningful to some of you than to others. Some of what I say, you may already have overcome, but before you dismiss a concept as one which you need not bother with, make absolutely certain that this is indeed the case!

15. Above all, remember that *you can do it*! There are many individuals out there who *have* done it. Most of them are not any more intelligent that you or I. (I do not, in fact, believe that there is any strong correlation between intelligence and success except in extreme cases.)

WHAT THIS BOOK CAN DO FOR YOU

Earlier I stated that we all have been exposed to different life experiences and, as a consequence, our various difficulties in the markets may be different. This book, therefore, cannot serve as a panacea, nor can it effectively deal with very severe problems of an emotional nature. In such cases, I recommend you consult a mental health professional. This book cannot and does not render psychological services. There is a fine line between what is considered psychological service and advice. My suggestions and directions in this book will help you get started on the road to self-improvement. What I am working with is primarily *behavior* not psychology. It is often possible to change behavior without any major shift in psychological structure. Once behavior changes, internal factors can also change. *There are many who will disagree with this last statement.* This statement epitomizes the major split between behaviorists (i.e., those who believe that all of life is understandable in terms of overt behavior) and the so-called humanists (those who believe that in order to change external behavior, internal forces must be understood, analyzed, and changed). I will deal with these viewpoints later on.

What this book will *not* do is "psychoanalyze" you, assess your personality problems, or help you with emotional problems. This book does not offer psychological or psychiatric advice. What this book *will* do for you, is provide a framework for understanding investor behavior and attitudes in the various markets (i.e., futures, stocks, options, etc.). By examining losses, profits, methods of responding to market developments, systems, signals, brokers, news, and personal motivation, the book will help you eliminate those responses which are counterproductive (i.e., resulting in losses) and replace them with profitable behaviors.

This book can also stimulate you toward more reading and more understanding of your investment and trading behavior. Even if this book does not prompt any change but merely motivates a majority of readers to move in a positive direction, then my work will have been done. To a great extent, you will get out of this book what you put into it. Those who read it lightly, take its suggestions and analyses lightly, and explore their market behaviors superficially will only benefit lightly. On the other hand, those who take time, follow the 15 suggestions outlined earlier in this chapter, and intensely assess their market attitudes and behaviors will benefit most. You may call me mercenary, but I would prefer to measure the benefits of this book monetarily. If, after spending some time with this book and, if after applying the principles toward changing investment behaviors, you show more profits, then you have achieved the goal. Once on the right track, you can maintain the proper direction and increase your speed. My goal is merely to point the way.

Finally, I do not want to give the impression that my way is the only way. There are many roads by which you can travel on the way to success. Some are more readily traversed than others;

some are more direct than others; some are longer; some shorter, some uncharted, some safe, and others swollen with danger. The way I will show you is one which I have developed. It is merely one of the many paths your vehicle can travel.

2

Investor Behavior: Learned or Genetic?

Many years ago I was a fan of the "Three Stooges" comedy team. I am certain that many of you have seen their amusing films, and I am certain that many of you have found them just as entertaining as I have. Comedy is often a good method of dealing with and expressing significant social and personal problems in a palatable way. This makes such problems less threatening and, therefore, more easily solved. The comedy of the Three Stooges has great social comment. This was true not only during its time, but today as well. You may wonder what the Three Stooges brand of comedy may have to do with trader and investor behavior. Although many investors do indeed act like "stooges," one particular comedy sketch performed by the group drives home a major point in relation to investor behavior and related success.

The routine begins with two professors arguing about the importance of heredity versus the importance of environment on man's social behavior. One of the professors contends that most human behavior is the result of genetic predisposition, while the other argues that environmental factors, learning, and social forces are the most significant determinants of behavior. One claims that he can take an individual "from the lowest walk of life" and transform him into a functioning, worthwhile human being through training and education. Enter the Three Stooges. Several highly amusing scenes follow which depict our subjects in training. The short film concludes with a coming out party for our trainees. All begins well. An almost miraculous transformation appears to have taken place. The trainees are suave, sophisticated, polite, and well-dressed. Slowly, as the pressure of the evening begins to mount and the subjects are exposed to old temptations, their behavior begins to deteriorate. However, the Stooges are not the only ones whose behavior regresses. Within a matter of minutes, the entire crowd becomes unruly. Supposedly cultured individuals follow the Stooges' lead and begin throwing pies and acting like fools. But the crowd is having a wonderful time. They're enjoying themselves immensely, perhaps, more so than ever before.

The situation depicted in this comic sketch has great significance and commentary about the human condition. Although it may be true that humans are a product of their environment and that they are easily influenced by learning and society, there are a number of basic emotions and behaviors which are likely the result of genetic factors. These basic emotions are capable of surfacing during times of intense personal and/or social pressure. In the party scene, people who had "good upbringing" were adversely influenced by the presence of three individuals whose behavior was most unruly and socially unacceptable. The implications for the investor are significant. How does this little comedy piece relate to the origin and development of investor behavior? Here are the analogies I have drawn:

1. We are all born with certain instincts and primary needs. As learning and socialization shape our behavioral repertoires, these basic needs are expressed in socially acceptable ways.

2. Although the social facade is always present, it can, under certain conditions, be penetrated and, although the learning may indeed have been strong, basic emotions take hold.

3. In the "Three Stooges" piece, the decision as to which is more important, heredity or environment, becomes a moot point. It is clearly demonstrated that *heredity and environment*

are always at work jointly. We cannot ignore the value of one in preference to the other. In the case of this story, there was a most interesting regression. Those who had the good social upbringing and supposedly "good" genetics regressed to a lower level of behavior, while those who had supposedly poor upbringing and "poor" genes were able to raise their status by education, but they also regressed under pressure. Essentially, the story tells me that none of us are immune from the potential danger of emotional response regardless of who our parents may be, what our gene pool may have been, what our education was, and regardless of our social class, we can and will respond emotionally when under pressure.

Investors and futures traders are especially vulnerable to emotional response. Food and territorial struggles of the Stone Age have been replaced by financial struggles of the Space Age. Naturally, the struggle for wealth must be accompanied by considerable emotion. These emotions can cloud judgment since financial security is, to a great extent, a primary need. How can the traders keep emotions at bay while making effective and profitable decisions? The answer to this question is twofold: *first*, we must understand the origin and development of behaviors. In order to do this we must define precisely which behaviors we are attempting to understand and change. We must also define the precise manner in which they are counterproductive or in which they either limit profits or aggravate losses. *Second*, we must show how these behaviors can be changed and what we must do to change them. This chapter will deal with the former; other chapters will deal with the latter. It is relatively simple to diagnose a problem. It is much more difficult to change behavior which has become problematic. There are many wrong behaviors and only a few right ones. I categorize good and bad as profitable or unprofitable. I do not mean to infer that there is some moral significance to these terms in relation to their profitability or lack thereof. We will soon examine how behaviors originate and develop. First, however, let's take a close look at precisely which behaviors I am talking about.

LOOKING AT THE BEHAVIORS AND EMOTIONS

I have categorized behaviors into good and bad, or profitable and unprofitable. Figure 2.1 lists the major behaviors in their appropriate categories.

Figure 2.1 lists, not necessarily in order of importance, 18 specific qualities which can work either to the advantage of the inves-

Profitable Behaviors and Consequences	Unprofitable Behaviors and Consequences
Organization—makes work more efficient and actions can be taken more promptly	*Anxiety*—can lead to impulsive decisions not warranted by system
Self Control—avoids making incorrect or nonsystem decisions under pressure	*Impatience*—can lead to premature entry or exit of positions thereby increasing losses or decreasing profits. Can also cause too much trading
Confidence—helps trader believe in the system and thereby execute its trades	*Disorganization*—makes market system difficult to follow and can waste time which costs profits
Persistence—means that the trader will not be easily defeated	*Insecurity*—will cause the trader to respond to the tips and opinions of others thereby creating losses or limiting profits
Contrary Thinking—will avoid the pitfalls of responding irrationally with the crowd	*Fear*—can result in signals not being followed or in positions being closed out too soon
Patience—will give signals and trading methods time to work before running scared	*Greed*—causes positions to be held too long or too many positions to be held at one time
Flexibility—the ability to adapt to different types of markets with different systems	*Overconfidence* is actually a defense for lack of confidence and can lead to overtrading and risk taking that is not warranted based on trading system
Objectivity—the ability to act in accordance with dictates of your system	*Rigidity* will cause trader to be inflexible and not adaptable to different market conditions
Motivation—the mental energy and goal directed behavior that feeds success	
Positive Attitude—different from confidence this predisposes one to success (to be explained)	

Figure 2.1. Profitable and unprofitable behaviors in the marketplace

tor or to his or her detriment. The specifics of each will be discussed later. At this point, however, let's examine how these qualities can develop. What follows is a very quick trip through time, tracing the development of various attitudes and behaviors. There are many different theories about the manner in which behaviors and attitudes develop. You can well appreciate the fact that there are many different theories of personality and that the field of psychology has many varying viewpoints regarding learning and personality development. I have chosen to discuss the development of attitudes and behaviors from the behaviorist point of view. *The Investor's Quotient* contains considerable information on learning theories (Chapters 3, 5, 6, and 7). I will not discuss these in great detail here; however, you will come to understand them by way of example if you are not already familiar with behavioral learning principles.

HOW BEHAVIOR DEVELOPS

You might say that what I am about to give you is a crash course in child development, learning psychology, behavioral learning principles, and attitudinal psychology. Certainly, the logical place to begin our discussion is with the birth of the child. Rousseau theorized that at birth each individual's mind is what he termed a "tabula rasa" or clean slate. Upon this clean slate, parents, teachers, and society "write" rules and experiences by which the child learns and develops. The child grows, in effect, to be the sum total of his or her experiences. What comes out of the child will most certainly be a reflection of what goes in. As revolutionary as this idea was during Rousseau's time and as romantic as it may be, it is not entirely accurate. It has been clearly shown that even at birth, there are individual differences among infants. Some of these differences are significant. Each newborn responds slightly differently to stress. Some will show increased gastric activity, others will cry violently. Some newborns will show increased pulse or blood pressure, and others may show a more global physical response in which all psychological sectors are involved.

Therefore, there are *significant differences at birth*. These differences probably result in different reactions to stress for the rest of one's life. Reactions to stress are, in and of themselves, powerful forces which affect the development of attitudes and behaviors. Many individuals will shy away from situations which cause stress, while others will repeatedly confront such situations.

The first building block of personality development, as I see it, is genetic predisposition. I believe, however, that genetic predisposition constitutes only a minor portion, perhaps 10% of the overall picture. When it comes to investor behavior, environment is the greatest factor. Is it true that great traders follow in the footsteps of their parents? If this is indeed true, how does one separate genetics from learned behavior? It has been my observation that learning and exposure to various experiences constitutes the origin of most investor behaviors.

The mere mention of the word "genetics" has often prompted great debates and even violent disagreement among all manners and sorts of people. Before I get into any hot water or cold water, I want to be perfectly sure that my readers understand what I mean by genetic predisposition. Specifically, I am referring to the stress studies on infants mentioned earlier and to the follow-ups which were performed on these children. There is no mention or consideration of any other factors such as intelligence, and so on. This is not what I am interested in assessing, nor do I feel it is relevant. As a matter of fact, I do not believe that there is necessarily any strong correlation between intelligence as measured by IQ score and market success. There may be other psychophysiological responses which have a strong genetic predisposition. I'm not sure we know many of them, but at some point in the future, we'll have to consider these as well.

The second ingredient of behavior development is learning. From the moment of birth, learning occurs as a result of stimulus–response events. The behavioral law of learning states, very succinctly, the behavior followed by positive consequences tends to be repeated, whereas behavior followed by negative consequences tends to diminish (be extinguished.) This sounds simple enough, but alas, like most rules and generalities, there are many exceptions, deviations, modifications, and so on. Later on I will deal with some of the important exceptions and additions to this rule. What are considered positive consequences by some are not necessarily positive consequences for others. The behavioral learning theorist, therefore, circumvents this problem in a very clever way. He states that any behavior which is being maintained must have consequences which are, in some way, maintaining that behavior. Consequently, the behavior must be considered reinforcing (i.e., rewarding). Although the consequences of a given behavior may, in fact, seem negative, the fact that the given behavior is maintained means that there *must* be something rewarding or reinforcing about the consequences. *Keep this point in mind since it will have immense value in later chapters.*

If you are having trouble with this last point, then take some time to consider the behavior of children who act "badly" in order to arouse a response from adults. The response may take the form of disapproval, physical punishment, social consequences of various types, verbal disapproval, and so on. One would think that the behavior would diminish as a result of its negative consequence. But it does not. Why? Because in arousing the attention of adults, the child has obtained his or her reward. It was attention the child was after. What the adult thought was punishment was actually acting as a reward. There are many similar situations in our adult lives.

Learning develops in many subtle ways. Children take on attitudes, behaviors, and opinions of their parents. More often than not, both the parents and the children are totally unaware of the learning process which is constantly shaping behavior. This does not mean to say that all children will develop the same personalities as their parents. Were this the case, people would be very predictable. It is, however, to say that parents take a very direct role in shaping behavior. Any parent who perceives his or her role to be anything more or less than a very specialized teacher is either attaching too little or too much significance to the job of parenting. I maintain that the learning process is the single most important aspect of childhood development. Development of childhood attitudes, behavior, and opinions, in turn, affects perception and social interaction. These are the major constituents of personality. Personality is the ultimate expression of all ingredients which have been part and parcel of any individual's development. In other words, personality can be operationally defined as "a set of relatively predictable, specific behaviors and responses in given situations."

MANY INPUTS

There are many inputs which comprise the "personality formula." There are social, interpersonal, religious, educational, parental, and philosophical to name just a few. There are even inputs for which we have no names or definitions. With so many different factors all responsible for shaping, learning, perception, and personality is it any wonder that we are still in the dark ages of psychological theory? Perhaps one day we will indeed know how, when, and why the various inputs are responsible for shaping behavior; however, as things stand today, we are not very advanced in this area. The behavioral theorist, nevertheless, does not take this state of knowledge as a sign of defeat, nor, for that matter, do any reasonable professional psychologists or psychiatrists. They all accept our state of ignorance, and, in their own special way, advance theories of behavior. Some may ultimately be shown totally useless and incorrect, while others may be proven to be very close to the truth.

The sad news is that *we really do not know* what is true and what is not. Many of the theories are romantic and have face validity. Some theories seem improbable, yet they've gained wide public acceptance. The state of ignorance in human personality has, as you can see, opened the door to a veritable "smorgasbord" of theories, philosophies, therapies, cults, sects, factions, and groups. Each has its own claims to fame; each has its own loud voices, yet none can absolutely claim to have the ultimate answers. This situation may be sad, but it is true. It is particularly sad for the individual in serious need of help. Although there is no certain answer, I believe we can take a pragmatic approach to solving some problems by understanding that part of this state of educated ignorance is due to the fact that *there are so many diverse inputs which comprise personality and human behavior.*

What I propose (and what I have proposed for many years) is that we take a realistic view of the problem. We know the basics of personality development and origin; however, we become lost in the sea of inputs. Therefore, we should study the *outputs* and the *process* by which these outputs are formed in order to get an idea of the inputs. This is not a new approach. Behavioral psychologists and psychiatrists have been using it for years; however, they've used this technique in distinctly different ways. The psychiatrist may administer a variety of "tests" in order to assess the present state of mental health on a variety of predetermined scales, each of which is claimed to be indicative of underlying psychiatric process. By creating a diagnostic picture, the psychiatrist will, theoretically, be able to focus on the various *inputs* which have created the unacceptable behaviors or which may be maintaining these behaviors. By the process of psychotherapy, it is believed that the problems will be cured. The behaviorist or learning theorist takes an essentially similar approach, however, with several *distinct* differences. The behavioral technique also requires the use of an evaluation or assessment technique. This technique is called *observation*. What is it that's being observed? Simply stated, "it is behavior that is being observed." It is not a series of responses to questions about dreams, childhood experiences, fears, anxieties, sexual attitudes, or guilt; rather, it is an assessment of behaviors, their frequency, their precedent conditions, their consequences, and the conditions under which they are most likely to occur.

WHAT DOES THIS HAVE TO DO WITH INVESTOR BEHAVIOR?

Since investor behavior is a reflection of personality, the implications for the investor are immense. Here are a few things for you to consider based on the foregoing discussion:

1. Investor behavior is inseparable from investor personality. Investors are likely to act in a manner consistent with their personalities or with a given aspect of their personalities.

Therefore, if the major aspect of your personality is anxiety, then you are likely to be an anxious investor.

2. Investor behavior can be changed. Although the process may not be a quick one, it is possible to change behaviors if we make the assumption that they have been learned. We might say that certain behaviors can be "unlearned" while others are learned. We might also *replace* certain behaviors which are counterproductive with behaviors that are productive.

3. It is not necessary to embark upon an immense task of personality assessment, psychiatric evaluation, or psychotherapy in order to change investor behavior. While it may be true that certain investors will benefit from psychological or psychiatric treatment, I maintain that this is a totally different area of personality and that investors can learn effective investment skills and behaviors through a specific process which has virtually nothing to do with psychotherapy. Unless an individual has sunk into the abyss of chronic mental illness or is in a constant state of neuroticism, learning to trade and invest should be no different than learning to operate a complex piece of machinery. Do we need a psychiatrist to teach us how to drive? (Some might say that we need to visit a psychiatrist if we are crazy enough to drive on today's super highways!)

4. The answers to successful investor behavior are generally similar inasmuch as the same basic ingredients are necessary to bake a profitable cake. Different investors, however, as a function of different personalities and experiences, have different needs, strengths, weaknesses, and responses to given situations. It is, therefore, necessary for *each individual to take a close look at his or her own behavior*.

5. In order to *change* investor behavior, we must first observe investor behavior. We must then *determine what is needed*. Finally, we must *construct a program* by which the necessary behaviors can be learned or taught. Finally, we must also make provisions for monitoring investor behaviors to make

certain that effective behavior is maintained and that it becomes self-correcting or homeostatic.

HOW CAN THIS BE ACHIEVED?

You can see the conclusions I've just reached are based upon an understanding of the *process* by which investor behavior develops. This same process can be employed to eliminate unacceptable or losing behaviors and replace them with known winning or profitable behaviors. As an example, let's look at *impatience*, a qualilty which I covered in Figure 2.1. What can we say about the *impatient* investor? How can this be changed? How can we teach this investor to be *patient*? How can we learn to replace this counterproductive behavior with one that is profitable? Here are a few step by step considerations regarding this matter.

1. *First*, we need to determine whether the impatience (let's call it the target behavior or "TB" for short) is actually resulting in losses. *In other words, just because we think that a given behavior may result in losses, the TB may not, in fact, be causing losses.* Think about this for a few moments! There are people who have all sorts of "bad behavior" but, who, through *compensation* in other behaviors can overcome their liabilties. Some very famous people have had terrible behavior disorders, whether drug, alcohol, neurosis, psychosis, or other such problems. These symptoms were overcome by extremely strong qualities in other personality areas. This is a very important point and one which *I do not want you to forget!* It is very important, therefore, to subject any TB to the "acid test." The acid test is very simple to administer. Complete details will be discussed later, but a simple application of the acid test is to answer the question "is this behavior directly or indirectly responsible for losses above and beyond the normal system losses?"

If the answer is clearly "yes," then we have a problem which can be dealt with, further defined, and moreover, one which is quite likely to be responsive to the learning process. I cannot stress this point too strongly. People tend to become slaves to popular delusions and misperceptions just as they tend to resort to ethnic and racial stereotypes. It has been a popular, but not necessarily correct belief that all "bad" behaviors must be eliminated from your personality just as one might want to remove all visible dirt from dirty clothing by putting it into the wash. It is not necessarily true that all potentially bad investment behaviors must be eliminated. They may remain present, but subdued or diminished in their importance, they may be overcome by other, more important behaviors, or they may, in some cases, be directed into a productive, (profitable) direction.

2.   If, then, it has been clearly decided that our TB is *impatience* due to *the consequences of impatience in the investor*, then we take the next step which is to study the specific *conditions* under which *impatience* presents itself. In other words, the TB may not always be present. It would be easier to change if it was a constant behavior; however, we must specify the conditions which stimulate or prompt this behavior. By the way, it is also likely that we will observe this TB to be a problem in other aspects of this investor's life. We are not interested in these other areas . . . let the psychologist deal with them! Behavior is often specific to its environment or conditions. Children will, for example, be "perfect darlings" in the home of one set of grandparents, and they may become terrible monsters in the home of another set of grandmothers. Why does this happen? It happens *because behavior is often specific to conditions in specific situations. These conditions will either maintain, promote, or help eliminate the behaviors.* There will be much more about this later. Assume, for example, that the given investor with the impatience TB exhibits this behavior only when he or she is sitting in front of a price quotation machine in his or her broker's office. Assume also that it is discovered that he or she acts impulsively under these conditions and that the end-results are severe losses which might otherwise have been profits (based on the trading system being used). Many times this happens unconsciously. How would the investor know that this behavior was specific to the given environment unless he or she took a detailed assessment of his or her losses, their precedent conditions, and their consequences. Also consider this . . . assume that every time such a loss is taken, the broker (in the inter-

est of keeping his or her client) takes the client out for drinks and dinner (how about a little attention for bad behavior?). Better yet, how about the broker who feels so bad for his or her client that he or she spends several hours with the client at the office pouring over charts and indicators in order to find out why the client lost money? If this behavior occurs regularly, if it increases, or if it only occurs infrequently, but under the same conditions and with the same consequences, then we can safely assume *that the precedent and antecedent conditions must be changed since they are maintaining the behavior or making it worse.*

3. Now that some very specific decisions have been made regarding the precedent and antecedent conditions of the TB, we can make some changes. We should, in the interest of being thorough, also examine other environmental aspects of the TB to make certain that it is not happening in other investment areas as well. In terms of change, then, the most simple thing to do, and it is indeed a very simple thing, is to take the obvious action and to see how it works. If being in the broker's office, in front of a quote machine, or in close touch with prices are the conditions which stimulate the response called *impatience*, and if this response is maintained by the reward known as attention, then the investor must remove himself or herself from these situations. In so doing, the problem will be avoided. There are those who may now say that this behavior will surface elsewhere in order to compensate for its not being expressed. This is not *necessarily true.* Behavior theorists have not found this to be a big problem if change is properly instituted.

The previous discussion is, of course, greatly simplified, however, it should give you some flavor for the manner in which the process of learning can proceed in changing investor behavior. The chapters that follow will provide you with some tools for determining which behaviors are limiting overall profits, how they continue to exert their negative influence on your investing or trading, how they can be changed or eliminated, and how new behaviors, which may not presently be in your repertoire, can be added.

3

The Paradigm

I have taken a back door route to the model which will be employed in studying and changing investor behavior. The model or paradigm is no mystery. It has been studied by behavioral learning psychologists such as Skinner and Thorndike for many years. It has been especially successful in changing behaviors, and it serves as the basis of many learning-based approaches to psychological treatment. More important, however, is the fact that the learning model we will be using has been employed in extremely successful educational programs. It serves as the basis for programmed instruction, so-called errorless learning approaches, and a variety of computer-based educational systems. In effect, what this book is all about is education and remedial education—the unlearning of what is *not* profitable, and the learning of what *is* profitable.

There are five elements to the behavioral model which will serve as the core of my approach to positive changes in investor behavior. Figure 3.1 shows the model and the elements of this model. In order for you to fully benefit from the chapters and techniques which follow, it will be necessary for you to understand the model and how it is instrumental in the development, growth, and change of investor behavior.

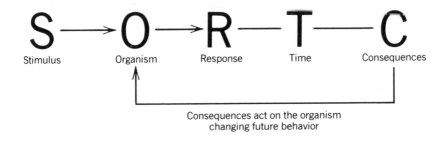

Figure 3.1.   The learning paradigm

Let's examine each aspect of Figure 3.1, detailing the role and definition of each.

Stimulus is the term applied to any condition, action, or environmental circumstance which affects the investor. The investor is constantly affected by all sorts of stimulation. We are only interested in those stimuli which are found to be related to the ultimate expression of investor behavior. They may be subtle; they may be obvious; they may be known; they may be a mystery, upon initial examination. Often there are many stimuli which act on the investor, and it is not possible to entirely separate the cause and effect of each. However, since we are more interested in final behavior rather than what prompts or stimulates behavior, we need not concern ourselves with determining each and every stimulus event. Another term that I will use interchangeably with *stimulus* is *precedent event(s)*. It says that we are interested in the event or events which come before a given behavior. In other words, we want to know what events stimulated the investor to act.

Organism is the generic term applied to that party on which the *stimulus* events are having their effect. The investor is, after all, nothing more than an organism. By using this general term, it is possible to examine all human and animal behavior in the same context. You may find it a bit offensive that I place all living organisms in the same formula. Actually, however, it is quite a good thing. It helps you put yourself in the proper perspective. After all, what are people? We are part of the animal kingdom and we are subject to emotion, rage, fear, possessiveness, love . . . virtually all the same responses shared by mammals with supposedly higher intelligences. Therefore, the paradigm refers to the *organism*. If it makes you feel better, however, just take a pen to Figure 3.1 and change *organism* to *investor*.

Response refers to the actions which are taken subsequent to the effects of the *stimulus* or *precedent conditions*. The response may take any of several hundred thousand or even several million forms. There are literally millions of ways in which an individual can respond to a given stimulus or precedent condition. In reality, however, there are only a limited number of sensible responses (appropriate responses). The manner in which individuals respond to *stimulus* conditions is, ultimately, what society uses as the guide for determining who is successful or unsuccessful; who is liked or disliked; who is elected president or garbage collector; who is mentally healthy or mentally ill; who is behind bars; who rules a nation; and so on.

This last statement has immense implications if you think about it for a few minutes. It's both simple and complex at the same time. When you consider the fact that the difference between incredible success and abysmal failure is due to different responses to perhaps the same stimuli, then you begin to realize how very important response really is. The statement is a very simple statement, but it has a profound effect on one who truly contemplates it seriously.

This book will, therefore, place major emphasis on response. What I will attempt to do is teach you effective response. When you really think about it, *response, effective response, economical response, appropriate response, timely response, energetic response, creative response*, and the many variations on this theme are the very core, the very heart, the quiddity of success in any venture, business, undertaking, or enterprise. Responses can be changed; they they can be redirected, reorganized, relearned, eliminated, circumvented, maximized, rationalized, or ignored. Response is what the markets are all about. One who has learned effective responses to given *stimuli* will show profits as the bottom line. Therefore, I cannot stress too profoundly the importance of this element of the paradigm.

Time is the next element of the learning model. Time is important, since it will either intensify or lessen the effect of behavioral consequences. In other words, if you do something right in the market and it takes five years for you to find out that this was the right thing to do, the learning that might have taken place may not be significant. By the time five years has passed, you probably don't even remember what you did. If, however, you had received immediate feedback and results from what you did, then you would have learned quickly as a function of the result of your behavior. Think about the importance of time in the learning chain. If you have children, or if you have supervised children (or even a pet) at some time, then you know the importance of immediate response. Assume that a child misbehaves. Will you respond quickly, indicating your displeasure? Will you say nothing? Will you punish the child in several weeks? It is important to have minimal passage of time between behavior and its consequences in order to promote effective learning. The ramifications of *time* are manifold. I will spend much time on *time*.

Consequences are, perhaps, the single most important element of the model, although it is obviously true that without all other elements of this symbiotic model, none would exist. Consequences are any events, actions, results, and so on, which occur as a result of the response taken by the organism. Consequences have a backward type of effect on responses. It is the consequence of a given behavior that will determine whether or not the response or behavior will occur again, how often it will occur, and in what form it will occur.

By changing the consequences of behavior one can change behavior. Behavior is either maintained, changed, strengthened, or eliminated as a result of its consequences. The formula is deceptive in its simplicity. Let's go back to the *impatience* TB that was discussed in Chapter 2. Let's assume that the impatience only occurs at the broker's office. One would assume that the consequence of losing money would be sufficiently negative to keep the investor out of the office. Yet, the behavior continues. What's the conclusion? The consequence of losing money is not sufficiently negative to result in change, and/or there are other consequences in the brokerage house that are offering greater rewards than the negative effect of the money loss. These rewards could be anything from broker attention, the need for socialization, an attractive broker of the opposite sex who sits at the next desk, or, in fact, the customer may be sexually attracted to his or her own broker. In other words, there are competitive consequences which may, in fact, be rewarding bad behavior. As with every aspect of the learning paradigm I've presented in this chapter, the ramifications, implementations, and possibilities of consequences are almost without limit.

I want you to appreciate the fact that in the foregoing material, we have dealt with tangible facts. We have evaluated and explained real behaviors. We have *not* dealt with unconscious motivations, dreams, fears, fantasies, and so on. We have stayed in the realm of real events and highly probable situations. All elements of the learning paradigm are capable of being defined operationally, in tangible terms. Two or more individuals looking at the same situation can easily determine and agree upon various elements within the limits of the model.

4

How Reinforcement
Works

We have already examined the behavioral learning law that very simply but clearly explains that behavior is maintained as a function of its consequences. The law is paradoxical in its simplicity. B. F. Skinner and other behavioral learning psychologists have demonstrated that virtually all forms of simple and complex behavior can be explained on the basis of this learning law. Furthermore, many systems of psychotherapy have since been developed to deal with behaviors which were once untreatable or were so chronic that progress would have been extremely slow. This does not, by any means, suggest that behavioral techniques are the only things available with respect to changing and/or eliminating negative habits. It does mean, however, that to ignore the principals of learning theory and reinforcement is to ignore a potentially powerful force in the area of behavior change. There is no simple answer to the complex problems of human behavior. However, I would be among the first to argue in favor of any scientific, moral, inexpensive, effective, and operational technique that has the potential to eliminate psychological suffering and improve the human condition.

The behavior of investors, as we have already seen, is quite a complicated thing. There are many inputs, outputs, sources of information, opinions, newsletters, brokers, and literally thousands of investments. There are virtually hundreds of things that the investor can do to lose money. There are only a few things the investor can do to make and keep money. Merely selecting the right stock or futures contract is not a guarantee that profits will follow. In fact, I am certain that most professional and successful investors would agree with my conclusion that selection is only the first step in a much more complicated process, and that it may, in fact, be the most simple step. It is rather amusing that so much time and energy are spent in pursuing the ideal stock or futures transaction. Such little time is spent in the application of principles which will make the probability of successfully completing the transaction in the stock which has been selected more likely. So much time is allowed to transpire between the process of selecting an investment and the process of concluding the investment that the likelihood for error is immense.

Considering the many different and complicated learning methods available to us today, the very simple application of behavior learning techniques to changing our responses is a very refreshing and pragmatic thing. In order to implement them successfully, it is necessary to have considerable knowledge and experience of the fashion in which learning takes place, the role of stimulus—response connections, and moreover, the precise fashion in which consequences operate to maintain behaviors.

At this point, I could take a very detailed side trip into the world of academia in order to outline for you the development of modern learning theory from its Pavlovian roots to its Skinnerian development. I don't believe this is necessary. Should you wish to pursue the matter in great detail, the additional reading suggestions I have provided will be more than sufficient to give you the knowledge you seek (see Bibliography). All I want to accomplish in this chapter is to give you some understanding of why the single most important aspect of the behavioral learning equation is the sector which deals with, explains, and implements consequences as a means of behavioral change. The most important thing to remember about any given behavior change is that it is not one single behavior. It represents the accumulation of literally hundreds, if not thousands, of other behaviors, all of which have been learned through the course of time, and all of which began from some very basic building blocks. Even a behavior as simple as opening a door, drinking from a glass, or turning on a light switch is complicated when examined in its many components. Perhaps the best way to appreciate the complexity of most behaviors is to observe a mentally retarded individual of adult age who cannot perform many simple tasks. This is very sad indeed, yet it is a picture that reflects the truly magnificent ability of the human brain to chain many small behaviors into one final behavior of great complexity. As long as you remember that the journey toward complex behaviors must begin with the first step, you will not only do well in understanding my discussions, but you will also do well in changing your own behaviors.

When the Soviet psychologist Ivan Pavlov was performing his canine conditioning experiments, he made some accidental observations which have great relevance to our present discussion. As you probably know, Pavlov surgically implanted a small tube in his subjects' salivary glands so that the flow of saliva could be diverted into a container and measured. He then proceeded to demonstrate that the salivary reflex could be brought about by stimulation other than food. When he presented his subjects with meat powder, they would begin to salivate. Just prior to presenting the meat powder, an audible tone or buzzer was presented. After many continuous presentations of the meat and the buzzer, the meat was eliminated and only the tone was presented. Of course, you know what happened. The animal responded to the tone by salivating almost as if the tone was meat powder. Pavlov called this the conditioned response. Pavlov demonstrated that animals and human beings could learn certain responses in connection with stimuli which were different than those that originally elicited the response. In the case of the dogs and the meat powder, for example, the animals were trained to respond to the bell or the buzzer as if it was meat powder. This was done by the proximal presentation of buzzer and meat powder.

In addition to these observations, Pavlov also noted some interesting sidelights of his experiments. He observed, for example, that when his subjects were about to be taken into the conditioning laboratory, they became excited and often showed minor salivary response not only to the experimental room, but also to the laboratory personnel who had been handling them throughout the conditioning experiments. In other words, there was a spread of learning which took place in association with previously established learning. Much work has been done since Pavlov's original experiments. Pavlov himself went on to propose many different theories of learning and human behavior based upon his model which is known as "classical conditioning." There have been those who have questioned Pavlov's work (i.e., Hebb 1943, 1949). Regardless of the criticisms, Pavlov's point is well taken, since it means that some types of learning, or what is also called respondent conditioning, can result in very interesting behaviors and responses which we might not ordinarily consider learned.

As an example, consider the following two situations. A student who has been successful in school begins to have difficulties with some aggressive students in the classroom. On several occasions the student is accosted and threatened. The other students want him to join a gang. After several exposures to this treatment, the student begins to fear and dislike being in the classroom and begins to feel anxiety each day before going to school. Before too long this very simple bit of learning has spread its effect by turning into a classic "school phobia." The child may then be referred to a psychiatrist who, not knowing the process of this current learning, will begin to look for answers elsewhere. The answers may not be found since the psychiatrist is not looking for answers in the right place.

This little learning situation is an example of how conditioned emotional responses can occur. In other words, the negative experiences which occurred in the classroom have now conditioned a negative response toward the classroom, even in the absence of the stimuli which originally caused the response.

As another example, consider the power of music to elicit certain types of emotional responses. You hear a song that arouses melancholy feelings. Where do these feelings come from? More often than not, if you recall when the particular song was originally popular and what you were doing with your life at the time, you will recognize the source of the conditioned response.

As a final example, let's see if we can relate this to the investment world. An investor receives a phone call from his broker with good news about a particular stock that he has bought. The call comes on a Monday. Assume, by chance, the next several Mondays are also days during which the investor receives favorable news regarding his investments. After several such repetitions, a very positive effect is created and Mondays will tend to elicit a positive attitude and positive expectations from the investor. In other words, the good news which was received by accident for several Mondays, has now spread its effect to that day of the week. Now, in the absence of good news, the investor perceives or experiences Mondays in a positive way.

Superstitious behaviors in the market develop in this fashion. In fact, this is the process by which superstitious behaviors occur in the noninvestment world as well. What do I mean by this? Let's assume that an investor subscribes to a particular chart service. Shortly after beginning to work with her new charts, several good investments are made. The classical conditioning here is that the investor has learned to associate profits with her new chart service whether or not her new chart service was actually responsible for generating these profits. Now, even in the absence of profitable investments, the effect and the response to the chart service will be positive *until the process of extinction occurs*. This process will be explained later. In other words, there is a superstitious belief on the part of the investor that it is the chart service which was responsible for her profits. In many cases, there is no conscious awareness of this process on the investor's part.

Another example is the "lucky broker syndrome." Some investors actually believe that they have better fortune with some brokers than with others. This may be true, however, it is not necessarily a function of the broker, but of the market and the broker–client interaction. On a number of occasions a broker may have had some very good stock selections for his or her client. These selections may have been made consistent with the existing market trend. They were not necessarily a matter of luck. A superstitious investor, however, attributes success to the broker and even in the absence of successful advice thereafter, the customer may continue to seek out advice from the broker, erroneously believing the broker is somehow "lucky."

Some investors acquire superstitious behavior through classical conditioning by several successes with given stocks, commodities, or groups of stocks. Take, for example, the situation of the investor who makes several successful trades in computer related stocks. Thereafter, the investor's automatic response to computer stocks is a positive one (whether or not the actual results are positive). It may take a number of bad experiences before the investor realizes that it was not the stock or stock group itself which generated the profit, but rather his or her *own* selection process which generated the profit. *In other words, it is important for the investor to know what caused the profit and what it is that he or she did to generate the profitable investment.*

5

Types of Investors

When I first began writing this chapter, the task of categorizing the many types of investors and traders seemed almost insurmountable. Then, as I began to logically sift through the available information on investor personality and behavior, and when I combined it with what I myself have learned in the marketplace, I began to realize that there were perhaps, 10 or so different types of investor personalities. I began to realize that it was possible to make some fairly accurate and specific statements about each type of personality. Finally, I began to realize that the knowledge of where you as an individual stand in terms of your "investment personality" may have significant implications for your progress, profits, and performance in the markets.

The insight or knowledge that can come from a realistic appraisal of your investment type or investment profile can allow you to take the necessary steps to ultimately change the losing ways which may be associated with your particular investment personality. Let me say, at the outset, that what I am about to present here is not the product of an exhaustive clinical search for investment personalities, nor, for that matter, is it the result of clinical evaluation or exhaustive testing. It is merely a synopsis of my experiences and observations of investors as tempered and directed by my years of study and clinical experience as a psychologist. Let me also inform you that there may be various types of personalities which I have either excluded (not intentionally) or covered insufficiently herein. If you find that this is the case or if you find that you can add something to our knowledge of investment personalities, then I would most certainly appreciate hearing from you. I am always looking to expand my horizons. Knowledge is ultimately to our benefit as traders and investors.

We have already seen that personality development occurs as a function of complex interactions between a variety of genetic, environmental, parental, and societal influences. The individual is exposed to all of these factors from the moment of birth. It has also been stated that individual personalities tend to be reflected in the marketplace with investors frequently acting in a fashion consistent with their overall personality. Generally speaking, a good example of this is the personality of individuals who are known as "eternal bears." Their attitudes about the direction of the market are not necessarily derived from any realistic interpretation of objective measures. Their opinions come from a perceptual basis of negative expectation which has developed as a function of learning experiences, most likely through their early childhood years and continuing through adolescence into adulthood. Generally speaking, such individuals tend to be morose, loners, somewhat antisocial, and usually cynical. They frequently have negative attitudes about progress in any way, shape, or form.

They tend to be politically conservative, often reactionary or right-wingers, and will ordinarily find many reasons to be negative, even about the most positive situations. In sharp contrast to the eternal bear is the equally unrealistic attitude of the "eternal bull." Coining the phrase of Candide's Dr. Pangloss, the eternal bull's attitude is simply expressed as "everything is for the best in the best of all possible worlds." Such an attitude will most assuredly result in problems, since such a person will frequently ignore the negative side of virtually anything. The eternal bull type is prone to make such mistakes as not using stop loss orders, failing to limit risk, accepting tips of all manners and sorts, and/ or trading on rumor in the face of technical or fundamental fact. Furthermore, such individuals frequently have excessive bullish expectations in that they often cling to positions much too long and expect prices to continue higher for indefinite periods of time. Eternal bull types tend to be ultra-liberal, progressive, upbeat, frequently overactive individuals who seem to have more ambition than they do brains.

THE ANXIOUS INVESTOR

In describing this personality type, I recognize the fact that the world is full of "anxious investors" and that anxiety is probably the single most common response to the marketplace. It would, therefore, be reasonably appropriate to say that all investors, to a certain extent, are anxious investors. As in the case of the other personality types which will be described, it is not the symptom's presence itself that creates the problem, but the pervasiveness or frequency of the symptom that results in unacceptable consequences. We all have a little anxiety, contrariness, bullishness, and bearishness as part of our personalities. What differentiates us from those whose responses are either unproductive or unprofitable is the intensity, frequency of occurrence, and consequences of these behaviors. It is safe to assume that somewhere in the development of every individual, certain behaviors have been learned or "stamped in" as a function of their reinforcing or rewarding nature. It is, therefore, also reasonable to assume that the anxious investor whose emotions and responses are differentiated from the so-called normal investor by virtue of their intensity and frequency has in some way received positive consequences from his or her behavior. Even if the consequences were not positive in an ultimate sense, then the results were reinforcing in the learning that took place.

Let's describe a few personality traits of the anxious investor:

1. An almost constant state of agitation and tension.
2. A need to get price quotations many times each day, in spite of the fact that the individual is not a short-term trader.
3. A need to talk to a broker frequently for reassurance on current investments.

4. The usual physical and psychophysiological responses associated with tension (i.e., headaches, gastric problems, high blood pressure).

5. Indecision in weighing the relevant factors in making an investment.

6. Spends a great deal of time discussing and working on the markets in an almost obsessive fashion.

7. A state of agitation reflected externally on the behavioral level as well as internally on the psychological and physical levels.

THE INVESTMENT GROUPIE

The Rock phenomenon of the 1950s through the 1980s provided excellent material for social psychologists about the manner and manifestation of group hysteria. During this period, many rock 'n' roll stars emerged as youth heroes, winning the admiration and dedication of thousands of young people. Styles of dress, mannerisms, attitudes, and opinions of these idols were often mimicked by their followers. To a lesser extent, there is a similarity between such rock 'n' roll star worship and investor worship of some trading advisors and newsletter writers. The term "groupie" is applied to an individual who literally follows his or her hero from one public appearance to another in order to keep constant watch on what the hero is doing. Groupies frequently demonstrate very poor judgment in pursuit of their icons. To a much lesser extent, I see the same type of behavior among certain investors and traders. They choose to align themselves with one or two market heroes, and they feel that these heroes can do no wrong. They frequently follow their investment heroes around the country attending lectures, seminars, and even radio and television appearances featuring their "investment God." It is not uncommon for an investor to try to establish a personal relationship with the individual being worshipped. There is a tendency to send gifts, letters of lavish praise, and invitations of various types.

What has just been characterized is, of course, an extreme example of the investment groupie. Yet, to a varying degree, many individuals manifest this type of behavior. It is very unfortunate that such things occur, yet I must give attention to this particular area, since it is, in my estimation, a significant problem of which all investors should be aware. I have already pointed out that what has just been described represents an extreme form of market hero worship. Please remember that there will be few individuals who fit perfectly into this ideal category. However, as with the "eternal bear," and the "eternal bull," this type of personality often occurs in varying degrees and upon a continuum of symptom intensity. In the long run, too great a belief in any trading advisor, broker, or investment analyst must lead to extreme disappointment. Logically, we all know that no individual is infallible, no newsletter always correct, and no trading advisors always make money. In fact, many trading advisors with good records are only correct 50–70% of the time. It is money management, the ability to take large profits and small losses, that differentiates successful traders from unsuccessful traders. Therefore, the hero worship of the type described is a most dangerous thing, and in its varying levels of intensity requires immediate rectification. There is nothing wrong with admiring a given market professional, nor is there anything wrong with attempting to learn from his or her teachings. However, if you find yourself strongly believing virtually everything this particular individual says, writes, or otherwise recommends, then you are probably on the road to hero worship, and it will be a rocky road indeed!

Who is it that is susceptible to this type of behavior? The same theme which we have seen in the other personality types described herein is relevant. Major elements of such personality types include:

1. Insecurity about one's own decisions in the market
2. Feelings of unworthiness and inability
3. Unwillingness to accept personal responsibility for decisions

4. The belief that there is an ultimate answer to investment success

5. A need to submit to authority in order to avoid personal responsibility for decisions

What's the "cure?" I believe that you will find many answers in what follows throughout the course of this book. You would do well to remember that most personality types in the marketplace develop as a function of learning, and that this learning is related not only to early childhood experiences, but to virtually all life experiences. As you will see later on, all behaviors must be evaluated in terms of their consequences and maintaining reinforcers. In other words, when you look at a behavior, don't look merely at that behavior, but rather examine its consequences. Evaluate behavior in terms of its consequences and you will understand it!

One final point before continuing our discussion of personality types in the marketplace is that it is possible for an investor or trader to exhibit many different types of personality traits without being a pure example of any one particular type. Such an individual has a more pervasive problem which will naturally require more assessment, a more intensive program of change, and a longer period of adjustment to new attitudes and trading skills.

THE ETERNAL BEAR

Now let's take another look at the personality traits and behavioral manifestations of the eternal bear. The "eternal bear" is an individual who is usually quite negative about most situations. This is an individual who will tend to see the bad in things as opposed to the good, the bearish opposed to the bullish, and the pessimistic as opposed to the optimistic. This is not to say that there is anything wrong with being bearish. I'm merely indicating that a persistently bearish attitude that directly conflicts with the actual evidence is the primary characteristic of the eternal bear. Even in the face of very positive news, the eternal bear's response will almost always be negative. There are other characteristics of the eternal bear such as, great pleasure in pursuing the short side of a market, anticipation of market tops and selling opportunities, clinging to a short position above and beyond the initial risk level and stop loss point, interpretation of most news as bearish, and generally negative attitudes about everything in life.

Generally speaking, the eternal bear is not a very happy person either in the marketplace or in life. While it is true that the eternal bear will have moments of great glory, the profits which are derived from the short side may very well be significantly less than the losses which are accrued by stubbornly clinging to the short side while prices move higher. You see, the problem is not that the eternal bear is bearish, but rather that the eternal bear *does not know when to call it quits on the short side*. The sad thing about the eternal bear is that many times an individual will be on the right side of the market at the right time and will make an exceptionally large profit in a very short period of time. However, the profit will usually be gone very quickly. The eternal bear becomes so negative on the market that he or she often continues to add to positions on a scale down. This brings costs down so low that when the market turns to the upside and a violent bear market rally occurs, most of the profit will be gone quickly, and the eternal bear type may end up with a loss. Another losing strategy of the eternal bear is to remain on the bear side for much too long while prices continue to move higher, usually well above and beyond the original entry point of the short position. Both of these conditions occur as a function of poor judgment due to perceptual set. As you will recall, perceptual set is the inability of an individual or group to view a situation in realistic terms, because of a predisposition or a vested interest in seeing a situation other than it actually is. In other words, the eternal bear has been trained to be bearish, therefore, he or she interprets things as bearish. As a result, even things which are bullish or contrary to the bear trend are not seen for what they really are. The result, of course, is usually a loss which was unnecessary, and very frequently a series of losses which were unnecessary.

You can see, therefore, that eternal bears are extremists who interpret most of life, which includes investments, in a negative fashion. These individuals are, therefore, prone to be bearish.

This type of extreme opinion and behavior tends to result in losses, as indicated, and is, therefore, unacceptable in the formula for success. It must be remembered that extreme behavior is what characterizes the eternal bear's personality.

THE ETERNAL BULL

Another type of extreme behavior in the marketplace is that typified by the "eternal bull." For the most part, the eternal bull's personality, attitudes, and behaviors are the direct opposite of those shown by the eternal bear. It is more frequent in today's markets to find eternal bulls since they are more strongly rewarded by society for their exaggerated positive attitudes. Everyone loves an upbeat person. The eternal bull is just such a person. Generally, the eternal bull tends to be positive about most things in life and more often than not unrealistically positive about virtually everything. For this individual, the tank is never half empty, but always half full. Even in the face of contrary evidence, the eternal bull sees all declines in the marketplace as opportunities to buy, rarely follows top loss, and is frequently prone to take tips, advice, "flyers," and news reports as indications to trade the market. You can certainly appreciate the fact that this form of optimism is counterproductive since it is not in tune with reality. It prompts buying rather than trading both sides of the market.

The important aspect here is that the eternal bull is an extreme personality whose unrealistically positive attitude can frequently lead to excessive losses. These occur from holding positions for too long, buying too much, and/or adding to losing positions. By virtue of an unfailing optimism, the eternal bull is likely to commit a number of blunders, all arising from perceptual set, and all directly or indirectly a result of unrealistic attitudes and expectations. When things are going well, the eternal bull is apt to add to positions without sufficient caution, and when things are going poorly, there is a tendency to hold on to positions much longer than indicated by the system which is being followed (or, I should say, *not* being followed). The eternal bull is well liked as an individual. In sharp contrast to the opinions often expressed about the eternal bear, the eternal bull usually has quite a following among friends. A positive attitude is quite convincing and appealing and gains many converts to the eternal bull's style of thinking and trading. Erroneously, many people seem to feel that an individual who is "so nice, so convincing, and so honest," couldn't possibly be wrong about the market. Well now, that's about as wrong as one can get! It is very important to understand that a distinct separation must be made between personality, market performance, and selection of investments. By virtue of the fact that positive attitudes and behaviors are much more socially acceptable than negative attitudes and behaviors, there are many more eternal bulls than there are eternal bears. This is why eternal bullishness is a rather pervasive problem in the stock and commodity markets and the reason many individuals are net losers at the investment game. There is nothing wrong with being bullish. There is, however, everything wrong with being bullish contrary to the market trend or, at the very minimum, contrary to signals which have been generated by one's trading system.

The two types of personalities just discussed, the eternal bear and the eternal bull, represent two ends of a continuum with regard to the market expectations emanating from personality types. These are, as I have stated, ideal types, and very few individuals will fit into the extremes. It is within these extremes that most individuals will be found. If you have the slightest suspicion that you may be somewhere at or close to the extremes of this continuum, then I suggest you either evaluate yourself on the basis of some of the questionnaires provided in this book, or that you sit down and make some notes about your attitudes in the marketplace. Examine the majority of your trades or investments, and examine your attitudes. Evaluate your ability to close out positions when your system so indicates. Make a decision about whether or not the type of behavior described herein may be limiting your performance.

Regardless of where you actually fall along the continuum, the ultimate measure of whether excessive bullishness or bearishness is your problem, must only be *performance in the market*. Performance in the market is operationally defined as the "bottom line." Has your trading been profitable or unprofitable? If the reasons for unprofitable trading can be directly linked to excessive bullish or bearish attitudes, then we have made a discovery which can be of significant value in the process of change.

These are two very rough sketches of two fairly obvious personality types, and I stress, as stated earlier, that these are ideals rather than actuals. One will rarely find an individual who has all the makings of a classic eternal bull or eternal bear; however, individuals can be aligned on a continuum. The extremes of the continuum are inhabited by those with the greatest potential problems. I have found that there are other major types of investor personalities in the marketplace. In the discussion that follows, I will attempt to give you some understanding of each major type so that you may evaluate yourself and determine how, and if, you fall into any of these categories. It is important to remember that any collection of personality traits is not necessarily in and of itself a bad thing.

I have stated many times throughout this book that personality and behavior must only be evaluated in terms of their consequences. If a given personality trait or behavior is not interfering with the investment process or results, then we can only conclude that the individual investor has adapted to these problems. We could also conclude that unless the individual so desires, or unless it is felt that the trading performance or the investing performance could be improved by making changes, there is not necessarily any need for improvement.

THE DOWNTRODDEN CUSTOMER

Another common personality type found in the stock and futures markets is what I call the downtrodden customer. The "downtrodden customer" is an individual who tends to be a net loser in the stock and commodity markets but who always blames his or her broker, either directly or indirectly. "My broker is no good," will say the downtrodden customer after taking a loss. "I wanted to buy," says the customer, "but my broker wouldn't let me do it." Such individuals will often run through a succession of brokers and brokerage firms, finding fault with each one for one reason or another. The excuses are many. If it is not poor execution of orders, then it is poor service; if it is not poor service, then it is slow service; if it is not slow service, then it is a bad research department. There are literally hundreds of excuses the customer can use in explaining or rationalizing poor performance. Few of them have much validity when it comes to bottom line performance.

The downtrodden customer, therefore, is merely scapegoating. It is unfortunate that many times such scapegoating will take the form of legal action against the broker or brokerage firm. The end result may be financial gain as a result of a lawsuit and not as a result of good investing or good trading. Many times such claims are settled quietly out of court in order to avoid immense legal costs. It is fairly easy to recognize the downtrodden customer. He or she has often been through a succession of brokers during the last several years.

At this point, let me give a free word of advice to brokers who may get involved with such a customer. I recommend you be most careful in your dealings with such individuals. Take great pains to follow all rules and regulations to the letter. Though I myself have had no direct experience as a broker, I have seen instances of the downtrodden customer making claims against brokers which are not necessarily justified. Downtrodden customers have a distorted perception of their relationship to the markets and frequently have a very high level of suspiciousness that is merely a psychological compensation for their own lack of ability. A handy scapegoat is often found, and this is usually the broker and/or brokerage firm with whom the customer is involved.

It is important to understand the psychological mechanisms which are working to keep the downtrodden customer on the defensive. Specifically, the downtrodden customer suffers from the following feelings:

1. *Insecurity.* Feelings of insecurity are generally the result of many years of unsuccessful investing. Although this indi-

vidual's original problem in the markets may have arisen from other sources, its ultimate expression is against other individuals as a means of compensating for feelings of insecurity and inadequacy.

2. *Scapegoating.*   Such behavior is not uncommon in the marketplace; however, it is usually directed against stereotypes and ordinarily has a racial, ethnic, or religious bias. Scapegoating is a common defense mechanism used by individuals who suffer from severe feelings of inadequacy and cannot cope with, compensate for, or otherwise adjust to such feelings. They, therefore, find it necessary to hold others accountable for their own failures and inadequacies.

3. *Rigidity.*   Such individuals also have rigid personalities. They are bound by certain fixed interpretations of reality which are generally impenetrable by logic or by common sense. Based on what I've seen in the investment and futures trading worlds, such an individual is usually so far removed from any sense of reality that it is unlikely any change will ever take place without a total refurbishing of personality.

THE OPINION HUNTER

Another personality type on the stock and commodity market is what I call the "opinion hunter." Here is an individual who makes it a lifetime practice to seek out opinions. In fact, this individual seeks out so many opinions that the net result is confusion. You have probably known such people. They spend so much of their time seeking out opinions from brokers, advisors, and friends, that there is often little time left to form their own opinions. We can certainly say that they are a veritable walking storehouse of information, yet when it comes to making decisions, they are usually quite lost. Frequently they fail to take action at the appropriate time. It would not be uncommon for the opinion hunter to maintain small accounts at several different brokerage firms, nor would it be unusual for such an individual to receive quite a few brokerage house and advisory newsletters.

The opinion hunter's situation is almost paradoxical. Here is an individual who spends a great deal of time studying the opinions of supposed experts, and yet fails to take appropriate action at the appropriate time. One would expect that for all of this individual's efforts, the opinion hunter would have excellent results. However, this is usually not the case. Why? What the opinion hunter does is self-defeating. By assessing the opinion of many different individuals and/or services, the opinion hunter is actually taking an informal survey of bullish consensus or contrary opinion. If the opinion hunter concludes to do what the majority thinks is correct, then what he or she is really doing is acting consistent with the bullish consensus or bearish consensus of opinion. If the experts are bullish, then the opinion hunter will be bullish. If the experts are bearish, then this individual will be bearish. Unfortunately, high bullish consensus among brokers and advisors is frequently negatively correlated with market direction. In other words, the opinion hunter is swayed by public opinion, buying when bullish opinion is highest and selling when bullish opinion is lowest. The opinion hunter is not a contrarian, but a scared and insecure individual who believes that the experts know best.

What type of individual is most likely to be or become an opinion hunter? I believe that the personality of the opinion hunter is characterized by the following basic elements:

1. The inability to make quick decisions
2. The belief that information and profits are closely correlated
3. The belief that brokers and investment advisors know best
4. The belief that the majority knows best

The basis for such beliefs is probably related to early childhood experiences, specifically, to a home situation which likely reflected similar values. Under the surface, there is probably the belief that "mother or father knows best"; that those in positions of authority should be consulted before any action is taken.

THE CONTRARIAN

Another personality type common to investors is the "contrarian." You may be surprised that I have included the contrarian as one of the personality types likely to have difficulty making and keeping profits in the stock and commodities markets. It would seem that the contrarian should be an individual most apt to make good decisions at crucial turning points in the market, decisions that are contrary to what the majority believes. This is, of course, true. However, there are two types of contrarians. The one type I call the "logical contrarian." The second type is most appropriately described as the "illogical contrarian." I use the term illogical to show that contrary opinion is not being used logically. The illogical contrarian is contrary for the mere sake of being contrary. The personality of the illogical contrarian is based on being eccentric, obverse, and unwilling to go with the trend. I want to make sure that you understand the distinction I am making. The logical contrarian is an individual who is perfectly willing to go with the trend as long as he or she does not have too much company. When the number of individuals, whether public, private, or professional, participating in a given trend becomes too great, then the logical contrarian begins to feel that his or her best position would be either out of the market or on the opposite side. Logical contrarians tend to use technical indicators and methods which will assist in their timing. The combination of these indicators help their market entry and exit. Logical contrarians have the ability to hold on to positions for as long as their indicators dictate.

The illogical contrarian, on the other hand, is a stubborn individual who is ordinarily so very rigid that, even in the face of evidence to the contrary, he or she will not yield. This leads often to riding losses for considerable periods of time. The illogical contrarian is most apt to disagree with everything you say, how you say it, when you say it, and why you say it. These individuals fancy themselves to be free thinking individuals who are unaffected by the illogical behavior of the crowd. Illogical contrarians have one major failing in that they do not recognize the importance of the crowd in helping to sustain trends.

What are the experiences in the personality development of the illogical contrarian which have been instrumental in the development of these attitudes? One thing we can look at is the fashion in which such individuals relate to society and how these attitudes developed from childhood experiences. It is not surprising to find that many of these individuals are acting out against authority and society due to very rigid standards that may have been imposed upon them by their parents during childhood. In other words, in their adult lives they are compensating for a childhood need to disagree with their parents. This need was probably aroused as a reaction to highly authoritarian attitudes of the parents. As in the case of all personality types described in this chapter, contrarians who are not experiencing poor market performance and who are showing consistent profits through the years, do not necessarily have to consider changing anything they are doing.

THE EDUCATED FOOL

Finally, I'll spend just a few lines describing an investor type I've seen many times in the last 17 years. The "educated fool" is an individual who has had many years of higher education. It is not uncommon for this person to have advanced degrees in mathematics, engineering, economics, physics, or computer science. Their intelligence is, no doubt, quite high. In fact, one is often impressed with their seemingly incredible observations about the market. The only problem is that in spite of their intelligence, education, and market observations, they are bound to theory and limited in pragmatics. They live in an "ivory tower" of how things should be, but in so doing fail to understand how things really are. Their potential can be used; however, it must be balanced off by pragmatics. Perhaps their difficulty is not due to any behavioral or psychological problem. Yet, it is important to remember that such people may prove to be big losers in the markets since they do not have the emotional or personality traits necessary to deal with the real world of trading. If you are a person closely tied to theory, highly concerned with the perfection or imperfection of the market, and if you cannot translate theory into practice, then beware!

I've sought to describe a few of the more common types of investor personalities. You may find that you fit one of the types perfectly, or you may find that you fit a few of them partially. Regardless, it is not as important to think in terms of diagnosis and definition as it is to think in terms of solutions. Naturally I cannot describe or do justice to all investor types. However, if you define the problem areas or symptoms you can work on each one using the learning approaches I've described.

6

Mob Psychology, Mass Hysteria, Contrary Opinion, and You

How often have we heard it said that tops in the markets are frequently made on bullish news and bottoms on bearish news? Few traders can appreciate the great significance of these simple statements unless they have directly experienced major turns in the markets. So important is the role of contrary opinion and mass psychology in the markets that a number of services both in the stock and commodity fields have made it their sole purpose to monitor the activities of the public, small trader, market professional, and newsletter writer.

It is the tenet of contrary opinion theorists that if a large majority of the public, professionals, and advisors are in agreement that a given market is either bullish or bearish, then it is highly likely that the market in question is topping or bottoming. It is not necessarily true that the top or bottom must be a major one (i.e., long term). It is not necessarily true that the top or bottom in question need last a long time. It is, however, reasonable to say that the higher the consensus of opinion, the more likely it is that the consensus is incorrect.

R. Earl Hadaday, in his excellent book, *Contrary Opinion* (1984), offers an intensive study of his bullish consensus figures, their meanings, interpretations, and implementation in the markets. Hadaday describes his techniques for establishing positions contrary to prevailing trends by employing the statistics he derives weekly from his survey of newsletters. It is clear, then, that contrary opinion and the assessment of bullish consensus are valuable indicators to the trader who is concerned about buying at the top or selling at the bottom. It is also true that there are timing techniques which may be employed in order to optimize market entry and exit. It is entirely possible, for example, that bullish consensus as determined in percent, bullish/percent bearish, can remain high or low for a considerable period of time before a market actually tops or bottoms. By establishing a position too soon, the trader might take a loss even though the market may ultimately move in the direction anticipated. It is, therefore, always a good idea for those who use bullish consensus and contrary opinion readings to monitor other technical indicators as well in order to optimize market entry. The specifics of trading with contrary opinion do not interest me as much as the psychology of contrary opinion, its statement about the human psychological condition, and its meaning to the individual trader at crucial turning points in the markets.

My goals for this chapter are, therefore, not to explain the particular manner in which contrary opinion is used, but rather threefold: (1) to understand why and how bullish consensus and contrary opinion function, (2) to provide some tools which will make it possible for the individual to determine when one is acting as part of a mob and, therefore, likely to take a loss, and (3) to provide suggestions which can allow the individual investor to overcome the intense desire to conform to prevailing market sentiment.

HOW MARKET OPINIONS DEVELOP

The market place has a reputation for bringing out both the worst and the best in an individual. If there is an individual who is conceited, too self-assured, or overly confident, then the market will most surely provide many opportunities by which these qualities can be tested and, perhaps, destroyed. Individuals who are meek, insecure, or unassertive can find cause for great confidence in the marketplace provided they can learn to trade comfortably. On the other hand, all of these qualities can result in failure and losses. The market, therefore, can make losers out of heroes or heroes out of losers. Hundreds of both varieties are made everyday. All who trade the market are well acquainted with its potential for creating winners and losers, as well as its concomitant ability to create and destroy great fortunes. It is no small wonder, then, that the market also has the ability to arouse great feelings of tension, anxiety, and insecurity among virtually all those who participate in it, whether daily, on an intra-day basis, or for longer periods of time.

Many of our modern day responses can be traced back to prehistoric ages when there was danger all about. Many times the cave man would be in fear of his life from dangers both human and animal. His security and existence were a function of his ability to overcome enemies, to hunt food, and to have shelter. Frequently prehistoric man banded together since there was strength in numbers and safety in large groups. This coming together of different individuals who shared a common goal served its purpose. Throughout history, great armies, nations, indeed, great empires have been created and destroyed by the ability of enemies to either penetrate or be repelled by the action of the group. It is, therefore, a natural human tendency to find safety in numbers, refuge in common attitudes and opinions, and security in similar thinking. Many societies, in particular, totalitarian states, dictate against independent or contrary thought and action. Such thinking is not consistent with dictatorial and communistic ideals. Even in Western society, where we theoretically encourage independent thought, action, and opinion, nonconformity and contrary thinking are often labeled eccentric, weird, irrational, psychotic, and otherwise unacceptable.

What is it about contrary opinion and bullish consensus which is so valuable to the investor? The simple matter of fact is that the opinions which are formed by the impact of news and/or economic developments, usually seem to be strongest toward the end of market trends.

An important aspect of bullish consensus is the distinction between opinion and action. *All too often, public opinion does not reflect the actual behavior of groups or individuals.* Rather, it represents nothing more than opinions. There is a distinct difference between opinions and action. Action is what causes tops and bottoms, whereas mere expectation is not a significant market force. This is why there are many times during which the consensus of bullish or bearish opinion will be very high or low, suggesting a move, but not, in fact, resulting in a move. It is important to determine what individuals and professionals are actually doing. In order to understand the distinction between opinion and action, let's look at the major groups of market participants.

There are essentially three types of individuals in the markets. These three basic groups are "players" who have different expectations, interpretations, and trading approaches to the markets. Although the three categories that I am about to discuss are very general, I believe they describe to a reasonable extent the major groups of market participants. The first group consists primarily of "professionals." These are people whose major source of income is derived from trading.

Generally, professionals tend to be buying when most people are selling and selling when most people are buying. Professionals also trade with trends, as long as the trends have not reached extremely high levels of bullish public opinion. Furthermore, professionals are generally interested in taking only a portion of each move out of the market. Typically, they are more interested in selling near tops and buying near bottoms, or in trading with trends, than they are in entering markets precisely at tops or bottoms. Professionals realize that the markets are like a treasure chest which opens on occasion and which must be "dipped into" only when it is open. In so doing one must take care not to become too greedy since there is always danger of the heavy treasure chest lid closing down upon one's hands.

The second group of players in the marketplace consists of "scalpers" or very short-term traders. These individuals are primarily pit brokers, floor traders, "upstairs traders" (i.e., individuals who own or lease memberships on the exchange but do not trade directly on the floor, but from an office, usually located in the exchange building), and a few astute individuals who trade primarily by computer from their homes or offices. This group trades primarily for the short term, usually intra-day, and most often they remain in trades for only several days at a maximum. They seek to trade with the trend or to enter the market when mass psychology has reached a fever pitch and prices are either too high or too low based on their short-term technical work. The common thread between the first two groups described is that *each seeks to take advantage of either existing trends or of extreme psychological reactions in the markets.* In other words, they *play the psychology of the market.* Frequently this psychology is taken advantage of on the basis of subjective feelings from the exchange floor or from technical indications which reveal the emotionalism.

The third and largest group consists of "the public." Although there are many different individuals in this group, they all tend to have the same responses, attitudes, and behaviors in the markets. They tend to make major blunders at significant tops and bottoms; they tend to trade against the trend, and they tend to hold very strong opinions at important market turning points. It is unfortunate that this large group of individuals tends to be the sustenance upon which other traders feed. *It's a sad but true law* of the investment jungle that the public, as a function of its typically incorrect emotionalism, is the basis for success for the other two large groups. This does not mean that all professionals or scalpers are successful . . . not by a long shot! There are many who have fallen by the wayside. What you call yourself and the group with which you identify is in no way an indication of how well you will do. *It is individual response, attitude, and behavior that counts!*

How can the individuals who fall into this third and most unfortunate group change their affiliation? The simple answer is "by changing behavior and responses." But this simple answer is difficult to set into action. It is, in fact, one of the most difficult things I have ever witnessed or encountered. I have some suggestions which will be of immense value in initiating the process of change. They are as follows:

1. Avoid listening to the majority of opinion. You can do this by closing your ears and eyes to most market opinions. This takes incredible discipline; however, if you can do so, then you will remove a major source of external influence.

2. Naturally, the many system related rules provided later in this book will be of significant value—read them, learn them, and put them into action. By being systematic in your approach, whether technical or fundamental, you will eliminate emotional forces which come from within yourself and from the outer environment.

3. Keep a list of your major market blunders—when, why, and how they were made. If you do so I am certain you will find an emotional basis for most of them! Once you are confronted with this evidence face to face, you may be shocked into reality.

4. Take time to study the history of mass psychology. Such time will be well spent. Read the accounts of the many panics, group hysterias, and mob reactions, financial and otherwise, which have characterized important turning points in modern and ancient history. This will further convince you that acting contrary to the mass behavior is usually best. It will also help you learn which emotions and responses are best avoided.

7

If You Don't
Like It—
Change It

We have already examined the very important role which learning plays in the development of human behavior. We have seen that there are many different personality types in the markets and that these personality types are characterized by certain types of behaviors. Although not all behavior is derived from a learning process, most behaviors, attitudes, opinions, and trading or investing skills result from the learning process. It is probably less costly, in terms of emotional and intellectual energy, to engage in profitable behaviors than it is to maintain unprofitable, emotional, and/or inconsistent behaviors. In the same way that the learning process creates unacceptable behaviors, the learning process can help eliminate and/or change them. In addition, the learning process can replace unacceptable behaviors with acceptable behaviors. Chapter 2 listed for you a number of characteristics which are closely correlated with successful investment and trading behavior. In addition, Figure 2.1 listed a number of behaviors which are counterproductive or unacceptable in a trader's repertoire.

In order to change behavior, we must now go back and refresh our memories of the behavioral learning model. You will recall that the model is quite simple. It maintains that a stimulus acts upon the investor, the investor responds, and, as a function of the consequences of the investor's response, the behavior is either maintained, eliminated, or changed. I have also pointed out, throughout this text, that in order to change a given behavior, the consequences of that behavior must be changed. Let's examine a very simple method we can use to change behavior by changing the consequences of investor response. Here are the major steps in this sequence:

STEP 1: DEFINE THE BEHAVIOR.   This step is more complicated than it seems. It requires specifying the exact behavior we want to change in the most precise terms possible. This means that we should make as concise a statement about the behavior as we possibly can, that we should state the environment in which it tends to occur, and that we should, if possible, also state the frequency with which it occurs, as well as its consequences. As an example, let's assume that the behavior we wish to change is "responding to market rumors." The operating definition of this behavior is "making trades that are not the result of signals generated by one's trading system." It is interesting to observe that we have, in effect, broadened our definition here to include input from virtually any source that is not the trading system itself. In other words, any trading decision which comes from a source other than the trading system itself is considered to be "tip" or "rumor." After all, is there any qualitative difference between various types of information which come from sources other than one's trading system? As a matter of fact, one could argue that any decision whatsoever which does not come entirely from one's trading system constitutes a breach of system rules.

It is a valid question to ask as to how we determined that this target behavior was worth changing. The answer is quite simple. By keeping a detailed list of trades, the profits, losses, and reasons for making them, the investor was able to determine that a great majority of trades which were not based on system signals turned out to be losing trades. Therefore, the only logical conclusion to reach was that making such trades was not in the best interest of trading profits.

STEP 2: DETERMINE THE CONSEQUENCES. You might find it a little peculiar that an individual would continue to trade on tips and rumors if one's results were negative most of the time. How could this happen? How could it be that someone would continue to make trades based on rumors in spite of taking losses on most of these trades? Why would one continue to do so? There are several forces at work here. In order to respond to these questions we must recall the role of reinforcement schedules. This has already been discussed in Chapter 4.

Let's assume that the behavior in question has been maintained on a random schedule of reinforcement. In other words, not every single trade which was based on a trading tip or rumor resulted in a loss. Some of the trades resulted in profits. Due to the random reward schedule it would be impossible to know ahead of time which trading tip would work. Therefore, one can say that tip taking functions on a random schedule of reinforcement and, as you recall, that behavior shaped or learned on a random reinforcement schedule is the strongest behavior possible. Simply stated, this means that tip-taking behavior will probably be one of the most difficult behaviors to extinguish or change.

STEP 3: DETERMINE PROGRAM FOR CHANGING THIS BEHAVIOR. There are several ways in which behaviors can be changed. It is not always necessary to work directly upon the consequences of behavior. There are two other techniques, at the very minimum, which could be used. The first is to change the stimulus or environmental aspect of a given behavior. How does this work? Let's assume that on closer examination of the behavior we are studying, it is determined that all the tips which were acted upon derived from only one source. This would be an ideal situation. It is rarely possible to pinpoint a stimulus event that has as much specificity as this, yet, for the sake of this example, we will make this assumption. Furthermore, let's assume the broker was the source of most tips which were acted upon. The procedure here is very simple now. All one needs to do is to change the stimulus event. In other words, the investor could reach an agreement with his or her broker that there will be no recommendations or tips made by the broker. This is, of course, a very simple solution. Unfortunately, the investor has not learned much by doing this. All the investor has done is avoided a situation that could very well crop up somewhere else or in an environment that was unexpected. Therefore, the first method of changing this behavior is not necessarily a very effective one in this case. It does have merit, however, since it could be included in an overall change procedure. Therefore, let's not forget this approach. We may be using it later on.

The second way to change behavior is to change the consequences of behavior. Is it possible to change the consequences of this behavior? How could we go about making certain that the investor took no profits whatsoever when he acted upon a tip or a rumor? Actually, this is rather ludicrous since the investor might run out of money by the time the behavior has been unlearned. What's required is a much more stringent approach which will bring about faster learning about the extremely negative consequences of tip taking. What might this approach be? The trader with considerable motivation to succeed could easily decide that if any tip-taking behavior occurs, then a self-imposed trading ban will be the consequence. Every time the investor acted inappropriately, a punishment of not trading at all for a given period of time could be self-inflicted. Generally, there is nothing wrong with this method; however, one would want to approach behavior from a positive aspect as opposed to a negative. In other words, the question now becomes, "Is there anything we can teach the investor which will compete with or otherwise eliminate this aspect of his or her investment personality?"

Another technique, one which appears to have more promise, would be to avoid dealing directly with the tip-taking behavior, but instead to reward or solidify behaviors which compete with tip taking. Are there certain behaviors which the investor could learn that would, by their very nature, make tip taking virtually impossible? This probably sounds like the old "walk and chew gum at the same time" joke, but, in fact, this is a very effective way of dealing with unproductive or unacceptable behaviors. How could we apply this procedure of strengthening a competing response? This would, indeed, be very simple. What behavior competes with tip taking? Very simply stated, following the rules of one's trading system will automatically eliminate all tip taking or trading which is not based upon the system. By its very nature, a trading system, is "systematic." The systematic approach leaves no room whatsoever for anything that is not part of the system. In scheduling a very specific set of procedures by which one will trade, the need to take tips should be automatically eliminated.

As an example, consider the procedures which an airline pilot must observe as part of takeoffs and landings. An investor preparing to enter the market is similar to a pilot preparing to take off. Prior to takeoff, procedures must be carried out, instruments must be checked, fuel and engine conditions must be evaluated, and the flight plan must either be known and/or filed. After takeoff, flight course must be monitored constantly in order to make sure that the vehicle is proceeding according to schedule. Flight plans must be observed and, if certain weather conditions develop, the flight plan must be changed. This would be very similar to a trader encountering unexpected developments while holding a particular position. If this occurs, then there are other procedures which must be followed. Finally, specific landing procedures must be sequentially executed in order for a safe landing at the designated airport to occur. In this respect, the analogy is also valid since certain procedures must be observed in exiting a position.

You can easily see that if all investment system signals and procedures are followed, just as a pilot follows procedures in takeoffs and landings, there is no room for extraneous input. In fact, although extraneous input might from time to time result in an enjoyable excursion or detour, it can also prove deadly. By sticking to some very specific rules which allow only slight room for deviation, tip-taking behavior will be eliminated. The question now becomes "how does one formulate, institute, and conduct a program based on very strong structure and procedures?" Details of this are discussed in Chapter 17. It is sufficient to say, however, that organization, specific procedures, check lists, constant monitoring, and immediate feedback are the qualities and behaviors which will virtually eliminate extraneous inputs of all sorts, whether emotional, social, irrational, or otherwise. What I am saying, in essence, is that the best way to avoid "bad behaviors" is to replace them with strong "good behaviors." By good behaviors, I mean behaviors which will result in profits. After a given period of time, the good behaviors will become sufficiently rewarding, financially, socially, and personally, that they will be maintained as a function of their own reinforcers.

The analysis which I have just completed on a very simple behavior has resulted in a very simple conclusion. It is, however, one which is exceedingly complex upon closer examination. What I have told you in effect is, "If you don't like something you are doing, replace it with something which will keep you from doing what you are doing." That is easier said than done. I have told you that this is the best way to avoid unacceptable market behaviors. The precise procedures for doing this will require considerably more discussion and, therefore, I have devoted Chapter 17 entirely to this subject. Before leaving the topic at hand, however, there is much more which needs to be said about three aspects of changing investor behaviors.

These three aspects are:

1. Identifying the stimulus and response correlates of behaviors
2. Determining precisely how behaviors are maintained
3. Determining the procedures by which they can be changed

IDENTIFYING BEHAVIORS, FINDING THEIR CAUSES, AND FINDING THEIR EFFECTS

The issue of cause and effect has for many years been an important one to scientists, sociologists, psychologists, philosophers, and writers. Without falling into the metaphysical quagmire of philosophical cause and effect, I would like to make a very brief statement about the behavioral point of view regarding cause and effect. I prefer to avoid saying that certain behaviors "cause" certain results. I merely look at stimulus–response connections and stimulus–response frequencies. I don't believe it is entirely accurate to say that a broker's advice or tip "caused" the investor to take certain action. Many things occurred inside the investor's brain and body following the broker's tip or recommendation. It is impossible to know all of the things which entered into the ultimate decision and, therefore, it is not possible to say that the broker's advice caused the action. The action was caused by the individual who made it. The only thing I am interested in is determining the correlation between certain stimuli and certain events or responses. Other than in very obviously reflexive behaviors, such as a knee jerk or an eye twitch, can we say that the stimulus caused the response. Therefore, I suggest you try to get away from causes and look almost entirely at correlations. By avoiding the issue of what causes what, you will automatically eliminate 90% of your work. You will not need to spend any time "understanding" why something is happening.

There are many who will disagree with me about this last point. In fact, I know there are many who will vehemently disagree with me about most of what I have just said. This is because what I have just said flies right in the face of most psychological and psychiatric reasoning these days. Let me say that I am not against determining causes for given behaviors; however, I am in favor of changing behaviors first and worrying about causes later. Most psychologists and psychiatrists feel that this is an impossible task. They believe that in order to permanently change anything, one needs to understand why it is happening. I don't agree with them entirely. I believe that eventually most investors will understand why they are doing something or why they have done something in the market. It is my belief that the process of changing behavior can begin first and that once it is under way with positive results, the reasons for why the old behavior existed can be explored in order to strengthen and maintain the change.

Although this is a very important point, I know that it may seem unnecessarily mechanistic. I know this because the idea of changing behavior without understanding what causes it is not a romantic one, nor is it one which gives sufficient "respect" to the organism in the equation. I have intentionally gone out of my way in this book to make the point that, at our very core, we human beings are slaves to many basic animalistic impulses, drives, motivations, and behaviors. Our social conscience (super-ego) keeps us from acting on these basic impulses. Our social conscience got there somehow. I maintain it got there through learning. When, as children, we were told that we could not do certain things, we rarely understood why. We were told why. However, we were too young to understand the reasons. Nevertheless, we complied because we learned that compliance was necessary in order to gain the approval, love, positive attention, and acceptance of adults. Later, in our pre-adolescent and adolescent years, most of the reasons why were discovered. The behaviors were solidified. I believe that investing and trading are subject to the same process. At first we don't necessarily know why we should do certain things in the markets. All we know is that they are the right things to do. We may even be given logic which supports these behaviors. However, we still don't know internally that these behaviors are correct. We have a "gut feeling" that we should do certain things, but we do not know how valuable these things are until we have *actually done them for a while* and until this process of doing has resulted in "insight."

I receive many phone calls from investors and futures traders who are experiencing great difficulties in the markets. They want to know why they do certain things, they want to know what causes them to do certain things, and they want to know how to stop doing these things. I can take either of several directions in responding to their questions. The first direction I could take would be to enter into a lengthy discussion of their motivation. After considerable time, they would probably feel better; they would have positive feelings toward me, believing that I had helped them, and they might even feel good about themselves. But what would they have learned? All they would have learned would be that they were doing something because of something else. Would they have learned any skills? If I took you to the store and bought you a bicycle knowing that you knew nothing about how to ride a bicycle, would I be doing you any favors? Absolutely not! If I gave you a bicycle and said, "these are the principles upon which the bicycle operates," and then listed all sorts of scientific explanations about how bicycles work, and listed procedures for riding a bicycle and so on, would I be doing you a great favor? Perhaps one individual in a hundred who had never ridden a bicycle might be adventurous enough, intelligent enough, and creative enough to take all of this pedagogical material and turn it into real bike riding. However, the notion that an individual could learn to ride a bicycle by following some scientific instructions is probably an absurd one. What must be done is to put the person on the bicycle, help him learn how to ride it, reward him when he is doing the right things, and make certain that when he falls during training that he will not kill himself. That's about it! After the bicycle has been mastered, a wonderful philosophical, existential discussion could be conducted regarding the metaphysical implications and manifestations of bicycle riding. Please pardon my tongue-in-cheek discussion. I want you to get the point. The point that I want you to get is that in my approach, teaching comes first and understanding comes second. Remember that I am not dealing with psychiatric or psychological disturbances. I am dealing with behavior. Perhaps it is true that to understand one's unconscious motivation will be of great benefit in the process of psychotherapy; however, we are not conducting psychotherapy here—we are learning a skill. Therefore, cause and effect are not the important issues for us as yet. What is important is to determine the stimulus and response frequencies and correlations in order to make some changes.

Another important point to remember is that as investors we don't necessarily have the time to engage in lengthy discussions about why we do certain things. In our society there are many things which we learn without question. Whether this means learning to drive an automobile, learning to obey the law, learning speed reading, racquetball, how to file income taxes, or how to run a business, there are proven successful methods and procedures. The areas of investing and trading are not necessarily as operationally defined in terms of successful behaviors. This is the case because very few individuals have taken the necessary action to make successful investing and speculation subject to the scrutiny and analysis which may yield the "formula." My pragmatic approach is, therefore, "if you don't like it, change it and worry about understanding it later." This might otherwise be expressed as "ours is not to reason why, ours is but to sell and buy," an expression I heard many years ago, but one which has stayed in my mind ever since. Therefore, if an individual calls me with a particular problem, complaint, or frustration about his or her investing/trading, my first question is not, "Why are you doing this?" I ask questions such as: "How often do you do this?" "How long have you been doing this?" "What are the results?" "What are the conditions under which you do this?" "How do you feel after you do this?" "What can we do to change this?" After we have answered these questions, and if we have time, we'll try and think about the many reasons why this behavior may have occurred.

As another point to ponder, think about the possibility that behaviors occur because they occur, and that there may be no other reason than this. I have found that chance occurrence frequently plays a great role in learning and that there is no way to predict when certain events may occur. It just so happens, however, that such random events often shape behavioral direction, good and bad, and that this is a fact of life with which we must contend.

One good technique for changing unwanted/unproductive behaviors is to first define them as specifically as possible, and then to set up a program for changing them.

The following examples illustrate this method.

Behavior: Buying or Selling on Rumors/Tips. *Definition:* Making investments and/or trades based upon information which is not derived exclusively from a specific trading system.

SUGGESTED METHODS OF IMPROVEMENT

1. Review schedule and procedures of order placement. It is very possible that you are not following your rules because your procedures are too irregular or lax. It is best to enumerate all the steps in your approach by using a checklist every time you trade, even after you feel that the approach has become "automatic." It is always a good idea to monitor

your market entry and exit procedures, even after you have learned them. This will minimize the likelihood of extraneous input.

2. Another solution, although not necessarily one from which the investor will learn anything, is to turn over your system to someone else. Naturally, you would want to select someone who did not have the same problem with tip taking as you do.

3. Another more creative solution would be to instruct your broker not to accept orders that were received during the day if the particular system you are using does not require orders to be placed during the day. This will effectively inhibit you from acting on impulse. With all the techniques described herein, rewards and continuous feedback are very important. Therefore, make certain that you let others know what you are doing and ask them to reward you when you have done well. The assistance of a broker is very important in this area.

Behavior: Overconfidence. *Definition:* Overconfidence can be expressed in many forms. In order to define this behavior operationally I incorporate two variables.

1. Taking a position in the market which is much too large based on your equity.

2. Holding a position for too long, contrary to signals generated from your system. This could include the target behavior "riding a losing position," but the reasons for overconfidence are somewhat different than in the case of riding a loss for failure to admit to it. Generally, the single most important variable in operationally defining overconfidence is trading a position that is much too large. The term "much too large" is not particularly operational, but as a guideline, I suggest that any position twice the normal size or greater constitutes a position that is too large, and hence, a position based on overconfidence.

Suggested Methods of Change

1. Perhaps the most simple technique for the habitually overconfident trader would be a very rigid budget administered
   by a second party. What this would achieve initially would
   be the limiting of position size. This, in turn, would allow
   the individual to make profits which might not have been
   possible previously. This new experience would also be rewarding, and therefore, a new behavior would be learned.
   The individual controlling the money could be a spouse, ac-
   countant, or broker.

2. Another technique for correcting overconfidence is the use
   of certain types of signals that will alert the trader when his
   or her attitudes are becoming overconfident. As an example, some investors become overconfident when they
   have taken several profits in succession. Others become
   overly confident when they feel that their system has generated an especially good trading signal. Yet others become
   overconfident when many analysts and advisors agree with
   what the investor is expecting. By examining one's past
   trading record it is possible to ascertain when overconfidence tends to become a problem.

8

How to Avoid Trading Problems

Perhaps the single best way to avoid serious problems with your investing and trading discipline is to structure your investing so as to minimize the probability of their occurrence. I have previously pointed out a number of ways in which "winning" behaviors can compete with "losing" behaviors. I have also pointed out techniques for minimizing the likelihood of errors. Many problems can be completely avoided if the initial steps taken are the correct ones. However, once an inappropriate or losing behavior has been incorporated into your trading repertoire, it is frequently very difficult to eliminate or minimize its effect. What I am saying, perhaps in a roundabout way, is that the best way to deal with problems is to solve them or prevent them before they occur.

Many years ago, when I was working as a clinical psychologist with institutionalized children, I observed a most interesting behavioral phenomenon in aggressive/disruptive children. I found that if I could break into the chain of aggressive behavior *before it had an opportunity to be completed,* my rate of success in totally eliminating that behavior was much higher. As an example, some of the patients when angry would engage in furniture-throwing behavior. The behavior was maintained as a function of its consequences which were, in a circuitous way, quite reinforcing. First, the furniture throwing was a release mechanism. By throwing the furniture, energy was released and frustration, which the patients had very few other means of expressing, was vented. Second, the behavior, which was usually directed at fellow patients frequently caused the other patients considerable injury. This resulted in great pleasure for the instigator, since he had achieved his vengeful goal. Third, the behavior received considerable attention from other patients. Fourth, hospital staff, who would then administer the necessary consequences, also gave the behavior attention. Since consequences of such behavior were limited in degree of severity, the punishment was rarely equivalent to the crime. Therefore, there was a net gain to the individual who had thrown the particular item of furniture.

Many of the staff felt that to administer consequences before the chair was thrown was somehow not fair to the chair thrower. I am reminded of the individual who is threatened with murder and contacts the police to report the threat. The police tell him, "I'm sorry, sir, there is nothing we can do until a crime has been committed." This Catch-22 situation poses an ongoing legal, moral, and ethical problem in our society. One cannot be incarcerated for thinking about murder or robbery. Even in cases where murder, rape, or other violations of the law have clearly been committed, it is frequently difficult for the legal system to administer the necessary consequences. This is at one and the same time both good and bad. Since it is part of the process of our democracy, it helps preserve our civil rights. On the other hand, many crimes go unpunished leaving the offender free to break the law again.

In the case of the furniture thrower, by a slight stretch of the "rules," one could reach the conclusion that attempted use of an item which is inconsistent with its intended use is a violation of hospital rules. Therefore, to raise a chair or other item from the ground with the intent to throw (as opposed to merely moving the item from one spot to another) constitutes violation of a rule. Now, the consequences can be applied *before the behavior is completed*. Thereby, the rewarding consequences of completing the behavior are avoided, making the behavior less likely to occur in the future.

Although the analogy is not directly applicable to trading problems, there is something to be learned from this small sidetrip. If you can stop losing behaviors as soon as they begin, then you have a greater likelihood of: (1) experiencing the positive consequences of successful trading, (2) eliminating any possible positive consequences of inappropriate investing behaviors, (3) making more likely the probability of future positive behavior, and (4) simplifying the entire investment program and its objectives.

Many times we have difficulty when translating theory into practice. Although something may sound good on the surface, its application in practice may be a more difficult venture. It helps to have an operational checklist. The general principles upon which a system of effective trading problem avoidance is based consist of the following specific elements:

1. Identification of specific problems in operational terms and a statement of precedent and antecedent events. By this, I mean listing conditions which tend to come prior to and after a given behavior.
2. A reasonable understanding of the reinforcers which maintain a given behavior.
3. Specification of competitive behaviors which can be substituted for the given target behavior.
4. Maintenance of a specific and operational list of system rules.
5. An organized and structured system for making the substitution in behaviors.

Probably the most important aspect of this technique is the ability to recognize the unacceptable behavior very early in its sequence. This can be done by a thorough understanding of the events which precede inappropriate trading behaviors.

CHANGE YOUR INVESTMENT HABITS—CHANGE YOUR LIFE

Few aspects of an individual's life are entirely compartmentalized entities. In other words, personality is a total thing and even though it may seem on the surface that different aspects of an individual's behavior are entirely independent of each other, this is not the case. It is virtually impossible for behavior from one sphere of an individual's life to be totally independent of behavior in other areas. Although you may not believe it is the case that behavior in the home can seriously affect investment results, I maintain that it is virtually impossible for an individual who has serious problems in his personal, social, or family life to be a consistent winner in the markets. I believe this is true whether you are an independent investor or market professional. I hasten to add that more important than problems per se, is the manner in which problems are dealt with. What is likely to have a significant impact on the trading performance of one individual will, perhaps, be virtually insignificant in its effect on another individual. Therefore, it is insufficient to merely examine an individual's life or lifestyle and conclude that this individual is having or will have difficulty in the market.

You can readily observe that the issue of personality and trading is at one and the same time a most simple issue as well as a most complicated one. The conclusions I have reached are that personality and performance in the markets are closely intertwined and that to completely understand these relationships is a most difficult thing. It remains true, nevertheless, that there are many individuals who on the surface, appear to have "problems." Some may be heavy drinkers, others may engage in other forms of drug use, while others are known to have serious marital problems. Yet, they continue to be successful whether in business, investing, or in most personal relationships other than their marriage. Why does this happen? Does this mean that problems are not important? Does this mean that problems can be overcome? Does this mean that investments are not necessarily related to personality and behavior? To answer these questions we need first to discuss the issue of "coping styles."

COPING STYLES

"Coping style" means precisely what it says. It is a style or manner by which the individual copes. Coping styles can be classified as either productive, neutral, or counteproductive. Another way of categorizing coping styles would be to say that they are either normal, neurotic, psychotic, or borderline. By borderline, I mean prepathological; by prepathological, I mean potentially problem causing from a psychological or psychiatric standpoint. Coping styles are the key to successful adaption in life regardless of which aspect we are discussing. It is certainly true that there exists a host of complex interactive variables of which none can be singly pointed to as the ultimate source of coping style development. The actual development of these important personality mechanisms is not nearly as important to the investor as is the fact that coping styles can be changed and that all individuals have the ability to significantly alter their methods of adapting to stress, change, and success.

All too often we tend to moralize or pass judgment upon the behavior of others as a means of making our own behavior more palatable. In the present discussion of coping styles, it is not my intent to moralize, nor is it my intent to tell you what is best for you. In order to remain consistent with the tone of this book, I will not reach conclusions as to whether particular behaviors or coping styles are morally correct, nor will I make any judgments as to whether I approve or not. As a general statement, I will say that any coping style which has potentially harmful consequences either to the individual and/or to those close to him (family and/or close friends) is one of which I personally do not approve. The ultimate resolution of the consequences which result from such a coping style is more often than not destructive. However, I consider coping mechanisms that ultimately have no serious consequences of the type just described to be perfectly acceptable without moral judgment.

It would be worthwhile to consider two instances in which coping styles are different in response to the same stimulation. An investor learns that a company in which she has recently bought considerable stock is rumored to be on the verge of bankruptcy. Assume that the rumor is also viewed with great concern by Wall Street and the stock begins to decline. Nothing, however, in the way of technical indications to sell or to sell short has been seen. There are obviously two choices for the investor. The first is to stay with her system and take no action unless otherwise indicated by the system. The manner in which she copes with the pressure of the rumor may either help her stay with her trading system or prompt her to commit an error. An investor whose style of coping with stress is to respond with logic, good sense, and systematic procedures will be much better off than one whose coping style is to become extremely tense. The tense investor will resort to irrational and nonsystematic behavior.

You can readily see that the issue of coping styles is a significant one. By changing one's coping style one can affect many areas of personality in a positive or negative way. This is not to say that making a change in coping styles is a simple thing to do. It requires a great deal of effort, learning, and in many cases psychotherapy. Due to the pervasive nature of coping styles in virtually all areas of behavior, change in one area is bound to affect the change in another area. This is true to varying degrees in different individuals. I have found that one positive fringe benefit of making changes in investment behavior and/or other areas of behavior is that their positive results will "spread." It is somewhat difficult to determine the precise reason for this spread of change, but it is most likely due to several factors. They are: (1) The individual has learned new aspects of change and is applying them unconsciously to other areas of life, with favorable results; (2) The individual's attitude has changed due to success in changing a small portion of behavior (this has had a positive effect on motivation and more positive feelings are, therefore, reported); and (3) The symptoms of change in one area of personality tend to be similar to those which affect other areas of personality. Without the individual's knowledge, more than one area of personality has been affected.

Because personality, behavior, investment results, success in relationships, success in business, and mental attitudes are so closely related to each other, it is difficult to affect one without affecting all others. Many times the effects are not known immediately, yet they are there and eventually make themselves known. Minor day-to-day changes will, of course, have nothing more than passing consequences.

9

What's Right
for You?

The world of investments was once a very simple universe indeed. In the "old days," choices were limited to stocks, bonds, real estate, various businesses, and limited trading in commodity futures. In the 1960s, perhaps somewhat earlier, investing became a much more complex task, and choices increased dramatically, creating a veritable supermarket which, today, tends to confuse and frustrate many investors. Contemporary investment and speculative vehicles open to the trader include such things as stocks, futures, bonds, warrants, mutual funds, options on stocks, options on futures, combinations of options on stocks, combinations of options on futures, futures spreads, options spreads, and several more areas I probably can't remember. To further complicate the issue there has been a great interest recently in short-term trading strategies as opposed to intermediate or long-term investments. Profitable short-term trading has been made possible by a combination of discount commissions and computer technology. It is now possible to commit a particular trading system to totally mechanical operation on an intraday basis. Instead of taking investor time to calculate complicated technical formulae, it is now possible for the investor to spend most of his or her time implementing decisions on the basis of signals and information generated by the computer. This has, of course, had a significant impact on all types of investments, making them more readily evaluated and increasing the total number of choices available to the investor. You can see, therefore, that in recent years the job of the investor has become a more complicated one by virtue of increased choices. Paradoxically, technological advances have, in a certain sense, made things more difficult as opposed to less difficult. The "old days" of active trading in the Dow stocks and a few speculative issues are no longer here. The 1950s and 1960s were, by comparison with today's markets, extremely simple and basic. While the total number of available investment vehicles during the 1950s and 1960s was significantly greater than what was seen in the early 1900s, the world situation, the free world economy, and the financial world were significantly less complicated than they appear to be today. Nowadays, the aspiring investor must make many choices, the most significant of which is the choice of long-term trading or short-term trading. Whether such a choice is made consciously or de facto, a choice must be made. Many investors do not, in fact, include the long-term/short-term decision in their list of alternatives. Frequently, such decisions are spur of the moment occurrences whose results are often less than desirable. A broker friend once told me his definition of "investments." "An investment," he said, "is a short-term trade which showed a loss at the end of the day on which it was established." Funny? Not really! The definition is more truthful than many of us would care to admit. What the definition says, in effect, is that many times an individual will establish a short-term position in the market, but, after a brief period of time (usually a day), the position shows a loss, and the decision is then made to continue holding the position because the investor is unable to admit to the loss. The investor, therefore, rationalizes or intellectualizes the losing trade by deciding to keep it as an "investment." I believe, therefore, that every individual should treat the issue of long-term versus short-term trading as a decision which must be made *prior to any serious entry into the marketplace.* I believe that failure to make this decision can result in errors which can easily be attributed to the confusion arising from failure to have clear direction on one's time orientation to the mar-

kets. I believe that lack of clarity regarding the type of investor
you are (i.e., long term, short term, intermediate term), can lead
to market losses by increasing investor confusion, misdirecting
focus on the markets, and increasing anxiety level, which in turn
can result in incorrect decisions. Furthermore, the type of information which one evaluates, the type of broker one selects, and
the schedule one maintains in researching trades and investments, are all part and parcel of one's time orientation to the markets. One of the steps which must therefore be taken is the
analysis of time orientation to the markets. You can well appreciate that this is a matter of individual preference and no two
individuals require or have an interest in the same orientation.
While some investors are looking for certain objectives in their
investment programs, other investors find these objectives inconsistent with their needs and reject them. The chronological age of
an individual can have a significant effect on the types of investments selected and the manners in which these investments are
maintained. An evaluation of your needs, goals, and investment
objectives is a good way to clarify your time objectives. You may
find that long-term trading is best for you. You may find that
short-term trading is best for you. You may find that a combination of short term/long term is best for you, or you may find that
having someone else manage your money is ideally what you
need. Regardless of what the ultimate conclusion might be, you
will never know for certain unless you take the time to make an
assessment of your precise needs and wants. In doing this, you
must remember that what you want may not necessarily be what
you need. Many times individuals are attracted to investments
and trading systems which are not consistent with their actual
needs but rather reflect a wish or a hope. In the investment world
there is no room for fantasy, wishes, or hope. These are all emotional considerations and have no place in the decision-making
process. As we have seen throughout the course of this book,
such emotions (and in fact most emotions) are counterproductive
to successful investing.

In order to reach productive decisions about the type of investor you seek to become, I suggest you consider answering the
following questions before you commit any new funds or addi-

tional funds to the markets. Remember to be honest with yourself in answering. Answer the questions with *what is* as opposed to *what should be* or with what your fantasy may dictate. Be pragmatic, realistic, and honest.

MARKET TIME ORIENTATION/EVALUATION QUESTIONNAIRE

1. *What Type of Investment Is Appropriate for Your Chronological Age?* If you are a retired individual with no source of income other than social security, interest income, and dividend income, then it is obvious that your decision must be based upon these financial considerations. If you are young and with a fairly good paying position and a reasonable amount of disposable income then you can afford to take more risks and, therefore, your time orientation can be shorter. If you are either young or middle-aged, in an extremely good position regarding your salary or income, and given a stable source of income with sufficient assets, you can afford shorter-term trading. I also believe that the elderly individual with considerable savings and a stable source of income can also approach markets from the short term if desired. Age, in and of itself, is not the only factor to consider. It is, however, a starting point.

2. *What Is Appropriate for Your Income Bracket?* Essentially, this issue was covered in point number 1. It should be noted, however, that although an individual with very limited funds should not consider short-term speculation, it does not necessarily follow that an individual with considerable funds must consider short-term speculation. In other words, income level is important, but interest and motivation must also be given their full input.

3. *What Are Your Interests?* Be true to yourself. If you believe that you are at heart a speculator with virtually no interest in holding investments for more than several days or weeks, I believe that you should admit to these feelings and desires, but rather than put them into action, evaluate them logically on the basis of other questions in this brief assessment. Earlier I said that what you want is not necessarily what you need. It is also true that what you want is precisely what you need. You must make the ultimate decision based on many variables, including your wants and desires. However, your wants and desires are not and should not constitute a major aspect of your decision.

4.   *What Are Your Skills?* Have you found that you are particularly skillfull at selecting long-term investments? Have you found, on the other hand, that you are particularly successful at determining where prices will go over the very short term? Have you developed a trading system which is particularly successful and suited to a certain type of investment? Take all of these factors into consideration because they constitute one of the resources that will be available to you in your investment/trading program. It is important to determine your skills in making your final decision.

5.   *How Have You Done in the Past?* Have you found that certain types of trading or investing are more suited to your pocketbook or temperament? If, for example, you have been very successful with long-term trading in stocks, but have showed virtually nothing but loss in short-term investing in commodities, then the decision has been made for you. One of the most important rules in playing any game, whether sports, interpersonal, or investments, is to play to your strengths, not your weaknesses. Capitalize upon what you have done best in the past and develop that resource since this is where your energy is most likely to return its greatest profit.

6.   *How Much Time Do You Have to Commit to Your Program?* This is a very important consideration. Many short-term trading programs require intensive time input whereas long-term or intermediate-term programs require considerably less dedication. To attempt short-term trading without having sufficient time to research, analyze, and implement trading decisions is a totally inappropriate and self-destructive goal. What you do in the marketplace must be consistent with the amount of time you have available for such purposes. If you spread yourself too thin you will end up showing losses for your efforts. Be realistic!

7. *Consider Your Goals.*   Are you interested in creating income from your investments or are you more interested in capital gains? Income in the form of dividends from stocks or bonds necessarily limits the type of investment you will make as well as the length of time it will be held. If, however, capital gains are more in keeping with your ultimate goals, then you may indulge in short-term and intermediate-term trading. While considering your goals, you should also take an assessment of your income tax situation to determine if this is an important factor to your time orientation to the marketplace.

8. *Why Do the Markets Interest You?*   You may think that this is an absurd question to ask. As a matter of fact, however, many individuals are not entirely in touch with their motivation for trading. On the surface they may believe that they are in the markets for the purpose of increasing their income. The sub rosa motivation frequently has nothing to do with what is believed on the surface to be the case. Many individuals are in the investment "game" for the excitement of the game. Their primary interest has virtually nothing to do with profits. Profits are seen as the score sheet of the game and provide feedback to the individual about how well his game plan is going. I do not believe that there is anything wrong with such an orientation to the market. It is important to remember, however, that if this is the game, then short-term trading must necessarily be the vehicle since it provides the fastest feedback as well as the most prompt evaluation of game strategy and techniques. Be honest with yourself! If the game is what you are in it for, then play hard and play with real money. Play by the rules and play for the short term since it will give you the fastest feedback.

There are probably other questions to be asked in making your final evaluation, all of which have to do with your personal situation. Your health, your marital situation, travel considerations of your job, your anxiety level, and so on, are all considerations. I have attempted to highlight all the major areas for you. Since I believe that evaluating your time orientation is one of the most important things you can do for yourself behaviorally and psychologically, take as much time as you need to answer the questions I have posed. To get started on the right foot emotionally and behaviorally you must know precisely where you are going. This evaluation can go a long way in helping you get started with the appropriate expectations and goals. Unrealistic expectations lead to disappointment. Disappointment leads to frustration. Frustration leads to an emotional response. Emotional response leads to losing behaviors.

10

You and
Your Broker

One of the most interesting aspects of the stock and commodity markets is the multitude of different broker–client relationships that may be encountered. Many times the relationship between broker and client can be the determining factor in bottom line performance. Many times misperceptions, misunderstandings, and miscommunications between the broker and client are responsible for sizable losses. Frequently the inability of broker and client to understand each other's objectives and intentions will interfere substantially with the relationship, creating disharmony and dissatisfaction. I believe that the relationship between broker and client is the third most important thing in the entire structure of trading (the first two being trader behavior and trading system).

There are tactics one can take in order to fully understand and develop the broker–client relationship. The first is very simple. It merely states that the broker will not be used for anything other than executing orders. To a great extent, the growth of discount brokerage concerns has been helpful to investors and traders since it has effectively minimized the importance of a broker–client relationship. Discount brokerage firms very frequently do nothing but brokerage. They do not render research services, they do not dispense trading advice, they merely execute orders. This may, for many traders, be a classic example of cheaper actually being better. As you read on you will find out precisely why I say this. Before we go on, however, let's see if we can clarify some common misperceptions about exactly what it is that a broker does. In the good old days before discount brokerage, a broker was often perceived as an individual who not only executed orders efficiently and promptly at the best possible commission rate, but also as an individual who rendered advice.

Generally, the period from 1900 to the 1960s was dominated primarily by brokerage house opinion and research. However, in the late 1950s and the early 1960s, independent research became more popular, and independent research organizations slowly but surely began to relieve brokerage firms of their edge in the area of trading advice. As the cost of filling orders grew higher and higher, brokerage houses soon found themselves charging higher and higher commission rates. A number of enterprising individuals began to realize that much of the brokerage house cost could be cut if they eliminated their cost of research. Some brokerage firms continued to feel, however, that research was important in attracting new business and, regardless of the accuracy of that research, they continued to fund large research departments at very high costs. These costs were, of course, passed on to the customer. In order to justify the cost, brokers working for the firm were (and still are) encouraged to be salespersons in their dealings with customers. In other words, in the traditional approach it is the broker's job to render advice and to make customers aware of various trading situations which, thereby, generates more commissions for the brokerage firm. This yields a return on their research.

In addition, many brokerage houses place (i.e., sell) large institutional offerings of stocks and bonds, secondary distributions, various types of investment programs, and everything from tax shelters in railroad boxcars to apartment buildings. High operating costs have forced some brokerage firms to take a back seat, dealing strictly in commission services and dropping research, while others have continued with research and advice, but at higher commission costs.

There are now essentially two camps in the brokerage industry. The first are the discount brokerage concerns. Their job is very easy to understand. They are order takers. They execute orders and they report back promptly to customers. That is all they do. When a customer enters into a relationship with such a broker or brokerage firm, the relationships and its parameters are quite clear. A customer is led to expect nothing more than efficient execution of orders. If an order fill is bad, unfair, untimely, incorrect, or otherwise improperly executed, then the customer will have just cause for complaint, and the customer and the broker should solve the problem together.

Some customers are better off dealing with a discount brokerage, whereas others have a keen interest in the research provided by a brokerage firm. There are many firms which maintain proprietary research programs, whose research output is exceptionally good, and whose trading recommendations have, at the very minimum, been no worse than those offered by others.

The balance of my comments about the broker–client relationship are directed primarily at individuals dealing with brokers who are in the capacity of rendering advice and trading information. Before entering into a relationship with a broker it is always beneficial to observe certain prerequisites regarding the relationship. It is often a good idea to interview brokers and to have a "trial" or "adjustment period" with your broker in order to make certain that the relationship is indeed going to work for both of you.

DUTIES AND PERCEIVED DUTIES OF BROKERS

Let's take a look at the duties and perceived duties of the broker. Typically the public perception of the brokers responsibilities is as follows:

1. To provide the customer with potentially profitable trading advice
2. To be available to the customer for price quotations

3. To execute and complete price order transactions
4. To provide support during difficult markets
5. To assist in planning trading decisions, policies, and strategies

Many individuals also feel that the broker should make good recommendations on a fairly consistent basis. Most brokerage houses sell their services to the public based on just such an expectation. Therefore, it is no small wonder that brokers are expected to give advice, and furthermore, that this advice be profitable. Brokers, however, may have somewhat different perceptions of their role than do customers. My understanding of brokers is that few can be classified in a particular role since they see their relationship with each client as being somewhat different. Brokers generally see their job as serving the customer in any reasonable capacity in which the customer wants to be served. Therefore, if a customer puts a broker under the burden of making recommendations, the broker will make recommendations. Frequently brokers make these recommendations based on the combination of their own market work, the work of various services to which they may subscribe, and the research which is being done by their brokerage houses.

Other customers may want to use the brokers for nothing more than a "sounding board." Most brokers are willing to serve in this capacity. Some customers like to use their brokers as "whipping boys" or scapegoats. Naturally, anyone but a totally masochistic broker would be unhappy to serve in such a capacity. In Chapter 5, I discussed the personality of the "downtrodden client," indicating that downtrodden clients were most apt to turn on their brokers. In such situations, brokers should act immediately to extricate themselves, before any additional damage is done. Other clients may wish to use brokers simply as order takers, order fillers, and providers of information. Within the context of reasonable brokerage services, I believe that this latter use is probably the most sensible, rational, and least likely to create problems. I will not preach to you about the type of relationship you should establish with your broker; however, I can tell you that certain types of relationships and interactions between broker and client can result in unpleasantness for both parties involved. Therefore, the relationship between broker and client should be structured as concretely as possible.

There are many different types of brokers, many different types of customers, and many different types of relationships. I recommend, therefore, that a customer in search of a broker first evaluate precisely what is wanted in a broker. After this has been determined, the individual should continue with the selection process by interviewing brokers. Naturally, it should be remembered that an individual who is only interested in discount commissions, and not other brokerage services, should not waste a single moment attempting to find a broker who will provide research services, "hand holding," and frequent price quote information at discount prices. If discount commissions are what you want, then discount commissions are what you should look for. Nothing more should be expected. On the other hand, if you are looking for a so-called full service broker, then I suggest you consider the following questionnaire as a means of screening your broker. It lists some questions as well as some answers to consider regarding these questions.

CLIENT/BROKER QUESTIONNAIRE

1. *Are You Looking for Discount Commissions Only?* If you answered *yes*, then do not seek to get anything more than discount commissions from your broker, and in your interview of brokers, you should look only at those in the discount commission business. Do not try to trap a broker into giving you discount commissions and trading advice since this would be unfair to the broker and may have consequences that are not to your liking. Therefore, if execution of orders is all that you want in a broker, all you need now is to find yourself someone in the discount brokerage business who has a good reputation and good financial condition.

If you are looking for a broker who gives advice, a broker that makes recommendations and provides you with information on the markets other than just price quotations, then you must look for an individual who has an established track record and who has shown results on paper or actual results for several years.

2. *Are You Looking for a Broker Who Can Trade Your System?* Some individuals have developed their own trading systems which, for various reasons, they cannot put into practice. In some cases, the necessary discipline is lacking, and in other cases the constraints of a job and/or travel make implementation of the trading system virtually impossible. In this case, the individual might want to turn the entire trading system and account over to a broker who will manage the funds.

There is nothing wrong with this provided you select a broker who can both understand and follow the system. In doing this you should have a written agreement with the broker detailing how the trading system will be implemented, conditions for termination of the account, and so on. It should be made quite clear if you do not want the broker to trade on his or her own advice.

Some brokers conduct considerable research into the market and prefer to trade on their own recommendations for the client as opposed to having the client call his or her own shots. Through the years some brokers have achieved admirable and consistent records. Therefore, you might want to consider working with such an individual. It should be understood that your input will not be necessary. In fact, in many cases it is undesirable. Money managers often prefer to have as little direct customer contact as possible. If you are willing to turn over complete trading authority, then you might also consider many of the managed accounts programs which are currently in existence. Some of these, however, should be checked very carefully for their performance records. There are many mutual funds which have achieved very impressive records of growth through the years and whose performance is likely to continue to be good.

On the other hand, you may wish to give limited power of attorney. In such cases the broker would call you before he or she made a trade. This would be particularly true in the futures markets, where such types of arrangements are quite common.

Regardless of the vehicle ultimately selected for your trading, the rules between broker and client must be very clearly established to avoid misunderstandings. The best way to achieve this is not only through the knowledge of what you want in a broker, but also knowing what types of services which the broker might render.

**3.   *Do You Specialize in Certain Markets?*   Some brokers have a special interest in certain markets and do their best work in these markets. They will place orders in any market their customers desire, but they do their best work in certain specialized areas. When interviewing prospective brokers, you should attempt to find out if this is the case, making note accordingly. There may be specific markets which you will trade and you may find a broker who fits the bill when it comes to an interest in the same markets. This could be very helpful, particularly if you will be using the broker in an advisory capacity. Another reason for determining the answer to this question is that you will avoid unexpected surprises.

**4.   *What Are Your Hours?*   Although the stock markets open at a fairly reasonable time of day, some of the futures markets, for example foreign currencies, open very early in the morning. There are some brokers who do not arrive early in the morning, and who, therefore, are not usually in the office for the currency openings. Some brokers, on the other hand, usually arrive very early in the morning and stay late in the afternoon until all the stock and futures markets are closed. Most investors and traders prefer a broker who is in early and who leaves after the markets have closed. *One of the most frustrating and disconcerting things any customer can experience is the inability to place an order due to the broker's absence.* Naturally, a responsible broker will make certain that someone else can take the order from you. However, people who stand in for a broker sometimes do not understand everything they should about how you trade, how you place orders, and what your specific needs may be. It is an unrealistic expectation to require that a broker always be on time and always be present, yet they should be there more often than not. These two qualities are so very important in a broker that every individual should make certain they are completely comfortable with the schedule their prospective broker intends to keep.

5. *Do You Specialize in a Certain Form of Trading?* Some brokers are technically oriented, whereas others look mostly at fundamentals. Some brokers are very heavily involved in computer trading programs, while some brokers have no interest in computers. Some brokers specialize in a particular approach to the markets such as cycles, point and figure charting, seasonal price tendencies, or Elliott Wave Analysis. If you plan to learn from your broker, then what you want to do is to select the broker with experience sufficient to help you meet this objective.

It is not absolutely necessary that a broker have the precise system orientation as you. You may be better off with a broker who does not understand your trading principles at all. In this way you could obtain a different perspective on your trading. You might find that you and your broker make a good team when you both agree on certain trades, having arrived at your conclusions from different market perspectives.

6. *Are You Interested in Long-Term or Short-Term Trading?* This is a very important question because a long-term investor who selects a broker with strictly short-term objectives could have some problems.

It is very important for the client and broker to have the same time orientation to the markets since major differences between client and broker could account for many misunderstandings. Brokers are inclined to be rather short term in their orientation and consequently, they may be prone to advise quick market entry and exit to their clients. There is nothing wrong with this type of trading provided it is what the client wants to do. Some clients prefer to hold on to positions for a long period of time, yet under the influence of their short-term broker, they may end up trading for the short term rather than the longer term.

The reverse can also happen. On occasion there may be a broker whose orientation is long term. He may end up with a customer who is interested in short-term trading. In such a case, the customer who is more interested in getting into and out of trades quickly might be inclined to stay in trades for too long a period. This might interfere with the overall trading program of the customer and could also result in some problems between customer and broker. There are many other possibilities in this respect. It would, therefore, be advisable for broker and client to consult with each other prior to establishing a relationship in order to determine whether they are compatible in their time orientation to the markets.

Again, you can see that lack of communication and incompatability can be very destructive in the broker–client relationship. In the early stages, it is the client who will suffer. In the long run, however, both parties may suffer.

More Things to Remember

There are some other things to remember about the broker–client relationship. I would like to pass along my experience and observations about the best way to deal with brokers. Brokers who are reading this book also take note. Here are a few do's and don'ts:

1. *Business and Families Don't Usually Mix.* If you have a family member who is in the brokerage business, I recommend you think twice before giving this person's brokerage your business. I'm sure that this comment will ruffle a few feathers, but, to be perfectly honest with you, I don't believe that it is a good idea for anyone but the closest family members to be involved in broker–client relationships. No matter how perfect people may think they are, there will always be petty rivalries and jealousies which will, in the long run, undoubtedly interfere with the success of both the broker and the client. Furthermore, I believe that privacy is a very important aspect of trading. I don't believe it is right for all members of the family to know what you are doing in the market. Nor do I believe that all members of the family should be aware of your financial condition, how well you do in the market, or for that matter, how often you trade. This is nobody's business but your own. By dealing with a broker who is not in the family, there is a greater likelihood of confidentiality. The confidentiality that you gain will, I believe, help you with your discipline. Although you may be attracted to do business with a family member by the lure of lower commissions or even "inside information," I believe that this is a classic example of something cheap that can become something expensive.

2. *Don't Do Business with Friends if You Want to Keep Them.* The same type of reasoning also applies to doing business with friends. If your friend becomes a broker, you should not feel obligated to give your brokerage business to your friend. I have seen too many instances of friends becoming enemies by doing business together in this way. I do not believe that friends can be involved in an effective broker–client relationship. There may be some friends who can also maintain a good working relationship as a broker and client; however, I venture to say that these are few and far between. More often than not, the same problems occur as have been previously described in regard to brokerage business with family members. One's personal business affairs should really not be that closely scrutinized by friends. We are, after all, human beings with egos and feelings. Petty jealousies, rivalries, and competitive instincts cannot help but enter into a situation, no matter how close friends may happen to be. Therefore, I advise against having your broker or your customer be your friend as well. I believe that only the most well-adjusted individuals can be involved in such situations without the possibility of negative consequences. These negative consequences have already been described.

Finally, there is a tendency for brokers to become friends. I would also discourage this. You may think that I am a bit conservative in maintaining these attitudes; however, I believe in the distance of business relationships. I have seen and experienced too many situations during my years in the commodity industry to let the learning go unexpressed.

I believe that your relationship with your broker should be formal, businesslike and reasonably distant.

I do not believe that a customer should be swayed by a broker; nor do I believe that a broker should be swayed by a customer. Each individual has his or her own job to do. Reasonable separation and distance can only create good relationships. Becoming too close, in my opinion, is a dangerous thing.

3. *Do You Want a Broker or a Psychologist?* Another situation I recommend you avoid is turning your broker into a counselor or psychologist. During times of stress, there is a tendency to turn to others who are close to the situation. Frequently, investors will turn to their brokers for reassurance or consolation. There is nothing wrong with occasional reassurance or encouragement, but before you go seeking these things from your broker, you ought to examine your motivations to make certain that you are not slipping into a relationship based on dependency.

Furthermore, you must be certain that you are not putting your broker into a difficult situation by relying on him or her for such assistance. There is a tendency for this type of relationship to perpetuate once it has started and I think you should be on the lookout for problems if you allow such roles to be taken. If you have the need for psychological assistance, reassurance, or counseling, then consult the appropriate mental health professional. Don't turn your broker into a psychologist or counselor!

The theme that has been running through all the discussions in this chapter revolves around three central elements. They are: independence; confidentiality; and self-awareness. These three qualities are not only important in the broker–client relationship, but in virtually any relationship between normal human beings. Let's take a look at each quality and see how it relates to the broker–client relationship.

1. *Independence.* One of the main distinguishing characteristics between market winners and market losers is independence. This quality has been described and referred to a number of times throughout this book. Independence functions in a very important way in broker–client relationships. First and foremost, it allows investors to make their own decisions. It is only on the basis of independent decisions that investors will learn what they are doing right and what they are doing wrong. Independence for customers also means independence for the brokers. It allows brokers to pursue that which they do best. Any dependency relationship, whether in the market, with one's children, in a marriage, with chemicals, and so on, has the potential for becoming a destructive relationship. I maintain that dependency will eventually lead to negative consequences. We all need to be a little weak occasionally and need a little encouragement at times. It is not a very good idea, however, to place too much reliance or faith on trading assistance from anyone. A trader's job is very lonely. Independence is paramount to success.

2. *Confidentiality.* I believe that it is very important to keep one's personal investments, specific stock or commodities selections, and economic opinions to oneself. Unless you are employed as a broker, advisor, portfolio manager, or economist, it is a good idea to keep your thoughts to yourself. By making recommendations to others you put yourself in a position of obligation. If your predictions are incorrect, you will have bad feelings and these could easily affect your performance in the markets.

Another danger in expressing your opinions is that some people will probably disagree with what you are saying. They may have good reasons for doubting your point of view and you could easily be swayed by their arguments. By making your expectations known, you run the risk of changing your mind. The job of selecting investments and trades is difficult enough. The job of putting your decisions into action is even more difficult. Why further complicate the process by making your choices open to attack? Why take the risk of creating or increasing feelings of insecurity? I believe that traders and the investors should do nothing to jeopardize their ability to translate their systems into action. The opportunity for error in the markets is very great. Even on an unconscious level, the reaction of others to what you intend to do can have an impact on what you ultimately do. Therefore, unless you are being paid to render advisory services or to manage the money of others, keep your opinions and actions in the marketplace to yourself.

Another aspect of confidentiality is the privacy of results. I believe it is important for all investors to keep their results private. Unless they are engaged in the business of managing money, investors should keep their performances confidential. Regardless of what your performance is, if you don't keep it confidential, you leave yourself vulnerable to ridicule, scorn, jealousy, and rivalry. Again, the issue is one of potential psychological influence. The less people know about what you are doing, the better off you will be. I have personally had experiences in all of the above areas. I have had friends become jealous or resentful and had other market professionals take issue with my trades simply because their own conclusions were not consistent with mine. Opinions make the market. It should be expected that others will disagree with what you say. On a visible level, many people close to you seem to be happy when you do well in the market. Yet, on an unconscious level there may be much jealousy and rivalry. I believe that these can be kept to a minimum by maintaining the confidentiality of your results.

How does confidentiality affect the broker–client relationship? The answer is simple. Ask your broker to keep your trades and results private. He owes you confidentiality. If you have relatives, friends, or business associates who are also doing business with your broker, you should be particularly clear about your demands for privacy and confidentiality. My reasons for saying this have already been discussed. I maintain that a relationship between broker and client is, in some respects, like a relationship between doctor and patient. What transpires is a private matter, particularly when it comes to friends, relatives, and business associates.

3. *Self-Awareness.* The third aspect of broker–client relationships, self-awareness, is important in all aspects of normal psychological life. By taking the necessary actions and behaviors that will keep your level of self-awareness high, you will be in touch with your needs, motivation, wants, and communications. Many times the messages between broker and client are miscommunicated as a function of different perceptions. Perceptions are frequently affected by one's level of self-awareness. In other words, you may be leading your broker to reach an incorrect conclusion about your wants and needs as a customer. You may be doing this in a very subtle manner by using certain expressions, by having certain attitudes, and by having certain responses to your broker's behaviors. If you strive to be aware of your sutble and obvious communications, you will avoid the trap of miscommunication. By keeping your self-evaluation and self-awareness at a high level you will avoid many potential problems between broker and client. This is equally true for brokers vis-á-vis clients.

11

Sex and the Market,
Sex in the Market

Although the ideas presented in *The Investor's Quotient* advanced significant new concepts and directions for most traders and investors, there were few ideas presented which attracted as much interest as those involving sexual aspects of the marketplace. Apparently, there has been no change in the human condition. Any subject dealing with the most basic of human instincts seems to attract great public attention. Perhaps the greatest response, however, was from the media. I have lost count of how many calls I have received from radio stations, television stations, newspapers, and magazines, wanting me to expand upon the topic of sex and the marketplace. My response has been fairly standard. "There is really not that much to it," I say. Sometimes I will answer, "I am not qualified to talk on that subject." In fact, I often refer them to a book entitled, *The Bulls, Bears and Dr. Freud* (see Bibliography, page 208).

The intense amount of interest which this topic has stimulated through the years has most certainly surprised me, but I shouldn't be surprised. We all know that sex is not only a great problem for many people in our society, but that in addition, sex is used in many different ways to motivate and/or stimulate consumer response. Whether in the area of fashion, retail goods, or food, billions are spent yearly on sexually motivated advertising. Whether you are an adult, child, investor, or businessperson, you cannot help but be affected by the use of sexual motivators in advertising.

Recently, I have even seen some very "slick" advertising for futures trading that seems to capitalize on the relationship or perceived relationship between sex, money, and the futures market. Given both the growing interest and active role of sexual suggestion in advertising, as well as in our daily lives, there is literally no escaping the effects of this powerful motivator. Therefore, this chapter will pay close attention to sex and the marketplace, as well as to sex in the marketplace.

First, it is important to establish some working definitions as to what is meant by "sex and the market." We all know that one of the primary human needs is a satisfying sexual relationship. It is not for me to determine what is right for the individual, in terms of a "normal" or heterosexual relationship or a so-called "abnormal" or homosexual relationship. The end result is that sex, in whatever form, means arousal and excitement for the individual. Let's examine the two aspects of sex in the markets. These two aspects are essentially based on two levels of consciousness. Level one is, of course, obvious or blatant sexual stimulation. Level two is unconscious sexual stimulation.

LEVEL ONE: *CONSCIOUS SEXUAL STIMULATION IN THE MARKETPLACE*

Assume the following, purely hypothetical, example: A male customer who is seeking information on futures trading visits a brokerage office. Once there, he is greeted by a number of attractively (even suggestively) clad women, busily running about the office performing their jobs. The customer could easily be female and the employees male. Assume, furthermore, that one of these employees is assigned the task of securing new account information from the prospective customer. My analysis of this hypothetical situation (whether ethical or not) is that sexual stimulation or suggestion is being used on a fairly conscious, direct, and ob-

vious level. A potential female client being interviewed by an extremely handsome male employee might also be subject to
conscious sexual stimulation. It is not an uncommon business
practice, particularly in sales, to encounter such situations on a
fairly regular basis. For many years the slogan "sex sells" seems
to have characterized a common, but not necessarily pervasive,
practice among those involved in the area of "high ticket" (i.e.,
large money) sales. Sitting in the solitude of my own little office,
I have been approached a number of times by female salespersons
who, in one way or another, use their beauty or physical attributes in order to maintain my interest in their product. I am not
here to moralize. I can, however, say that such practices tend to
get results more often than not, and that there are probably some
fairly unscrupulous operators out there in salesland who may go
to even greater extremes. I must say that in the futures and security industries I have not witnessed this type of selling and,
perhaps, only on one occasion, have I seen anything remotely
resembling this type of suggestion. We can quite safely say, therefore, that fairly obvious types of sexual stimulation are not used
with any great frequency in the futures or security industries.
This does not, however, mean that the markets are free from
more subtle sexual issues. Most of them, however, operate on a
fairly unconscious level. This brings us to the second aspect of
sex in the marketplace.

LEVEL TWO: *SUBLIMINAL, UNCONSCIOUS, SEXUAL ISSUES, AND MOTIVATORS IN THE MARKETS*

There is no individual in the field of psychology and psychiatry
who is more closely associated with the study of sexual development, psychosexual development, and human psychiatry than
Dr. Sigmund Freud. Freud originated and developed the concept
of psychosexual development. He went on to formulate psycho-
analytic treatment of behavior disorders through the application
of principles derived from the core idea that impaired or sub-
verted psychosexual development during childhood and adolescence were responsible directly and indirectly for aberrant,

neurotic, and/or psychotic adult behavior. The merits of Freud's work (or the lack thereof) have been contested for many years and will undoubtedly remain a heated topic of debate, not only among professional psychologists and psychiatrists, but among the general public as well. To many, Freud is an innovator, a savior, and a brilliant therapist. Yet, to others, he is a sinner, heretic, and colloquially, "a dirty old man." Sex, in any form, arouses strong feelings, responses, and emotions.

If we accept the teachings and therapeutic methods of Freud, then we have no choice but to interpret most investor behavior using psychosexual principles as the core of unconscious motivation in the markets. How does this work? Let's take a brief trip back to childhood in order to ascertain where some of these ideas come from.

The original Freudian concept of the Oedipal conflict originates from a fairly simple hypothesis. It is assumed that the male child enters into conscious and unconscious conflict with father as they vie for the mother's attention. The father exerts his territorial right and emerges as the victor. To the child, the father represents authority, the institution, supremacy, and the administrator of punishment. The father is often seen as more powerful and victorious because he happens to have more sexual prowess, experience, and certainly, more physical endowment than the male child. The male child, however, does not appreciate the fact that these things are normal due to the father's age. Furthermore, the child fears unconsciously that his father may attempt to end the competition by resorting to castration. Whether you can accept all of this, either in good faith or through actual experience or knowledge, this conflict (greatly condensed for our purposes in this discussion) characterizes the first serious psychological interaction between a male child and his father. The Electra conflict, between mother and female child, works basically the same way; however, it is the father's attention which is sought after, and it is the mother who is seen in the punitive role. (This, by the way, has always seemed to be a weak point in Freud's theory. Since there is no real fear of castration, there may be other issues at work.)

If we accept, on a very general level, that there is some sort of competition between father and son and mother and daughter for the attention of the parent of the opposite sex, then we can indeed make a case for early childhood experiences having a potential impact on the development of adult personality.

Without resorting to a radical application of Freudian concepts, I think it is reasonable to assume that in many cases there is psychosexual interaction between parents and children; whether these revolve around sexual competition or related issues such as autoeroticism, freedom of sexual expression, and sexual performance. The formula which governs such interactions, according to Freud, is that competition with the adult member of the opposite sex arouses real or imagined fears of sexual retaliation. These fears produce anxiety as well as a number of other psychological responses and neurotic manifestations. Unless these issues are worked out or resolved during childhood and adolescence, they may take a more serious form in adulthood. Relating such experiences to the investor, one could indeed envision a host of situations in which sexual development may indirectly be responsible for certain investor behaviors. These behaviors, which can be either productive or counterproductive, will be discussed later in this book.

Another area of sexuality in the marketplace relates to motivation. In this respect, subliminal or unconscious suggestion may be the force which is hard at work. In Western society, considerable value is placed upon tangible wealth and material possessions. These, of course, are acquired in a number of ways, each of which reflects the ability or prowess of the individual. For all intents and purposes, money in Western society is equivalent to power. There are many things which money can buy, some of which include the direct purchase of sex. I am not telling you anything new. This is something of which virtually every reader is aware, and it is certainly something that is very much alive in our society. Many times, relationships are indirectly purchased by wealthy individuals who use their money as influence. They surround themselves with attractive sex partners who may have no other interest in the relationship than the material benefits they accrue. Investing is frequently a vehicle by which wealth is accumulated. The roundabout equation, money equals power equals sex, is certainly not a far-fetched one. Although such motivation may not necessarily be conscious, there are probably many investors who are motivated to achieve success in the marketplace in order to ultimately act out their sexual fantasies through the use of the money which they expect to acquire through investing and/or speculation.

Another indirect influence of sexual motivation in the marketplace is the search for the "ideal mate." If we assume the idealistic fantasy that all people who get married must necessarily be in love, then we can only ask what it is that stimulates love.

What may attract one individual to another and what may perpetuate their relationship (culminating in marriage) may, to a great extent, be influenced by materialistic factors. The attractive young man who has no money is, to many women in the West, considerably less desirable than the attractive man who has money. Furthermore, an unattractive man with money, may in fact, be more desirable to many women, than the attractive man with no money. Men are also attracted to women of considerable financial means. In fact, such women are quite desirable and are often the target of many men who seek to marry into money. Quite naturally, it is important to hide conscious or unconscious motivation with love and endearment. I have found, however, that money is a great motivator in every type of relationship and that there are few "ideal" love relationships which do not, at some point, or in some way, relate to money as an important item. If I have burst any balloons, created any enemies, or touched upon an exposed or sensitive nerve, then I apologize to those who have been offended. All I can say in my defense (if it is indeed necessary to defend any of this) is that people are very creative when it comes to hiding the truth from themselves, particularly when the truth is either too painful, unromantic, or contrary to what society and religion teach. Not all of love is money, but in many relationships, money is *much more powerful than many of us believe, admit, or know!*

If we assume that "money equals power equals sex and love" is a reasonable and viable equation, then we can also assume that "investment ability equals money equals power equals sex and love." Through this roundabout equation, we can establish an essentially indirect and unconscious relationship between sex, love, and investing. For those with a penchant for romanticism, I again apologize for the rather crude and unfeeling equation I have just presented. I am quite certain that there are many variations on this theme and that the picture is not as purely financial as I may have presented it. There is, nevertheless, an element of sexual motivation which may prompt market behavior on a level which eludes the conscious awareness of most investors.

What can we then conclude about the sexual aspects of investing or speculating? I believe it is reasonable to reach the following very general conclusions:

1. It may be true that on an unconscious level, some individuals view their achievement in the marketplace or lack thereof as a psychological equivalent to sexual ability.

2. Some individuals who suffer from serious feelings of inadequacy may, in fact, compensate for these feelings by attempting to succeed in the investment or speculative worlds.

3. Some aspects of trading or speculation could certainly be viewed in sexual terms. After all, in our society, money is a very powerful tool. The individual with enough money can control many things. Much can be bought and sold with money. On an unconscious level, or perhaps on a conscious level, some individuals strive for success in the market because they feel it will increase their sexual opportunities.

I am certain that if one desired to do so, most investing or speculation could be viewed in sexual terms. I do not know, however, what good this would do the investor who has learned some self-destructive habits. The analysis of potential sex difficulty could provide some information as to why the individual is not as stable as he or she might be. It is, however, more important to benefit from understanding why and how certain behaviors are learned than before there can be a concerted effort to change them.

In conclusion, I have given as much coverage to the issue of sex in the marketplace as I possibly can without arousing too many negative reactions from one faction or another. The issue is very complex, significant, and emotional. Those who have reason to believe that their market behavior and/or performance are being affected by unconscious sexual feelings, motivation, or frustration should seek professional help from a psychiatrist or psychologist who specializes in this area. A classical psychoanalyst is, perhaps, the person you should consult in such a case.

12

Advisory Services: Pros and Cons

I've often been asked whether I recommend advisory service newsletters as a means of participating in the stock or commodity markets. I should say, at the outset, that I am probably the wrong person to ask since I am the publisher of three such newsletters. I will, however, attempt to be as fair as I possibly can with a clear conscience since I have forewarned you of my possible vested interest. The answer to the question as to whether one should subscribe to an advisory newsletter can best be answered by asking more questions. There are three basic issues involved in answering this query. First, I would ask whether you consider yourself to be a fairly independent investor (trader). Secondly, do you have the discipline to stay with an advisor through good times and bad. Third, are you more interested in learning about the markets from those who have considerable experience, or would you rather learn on your own by making your own decisions, having your own successes, and experiencing your own failures? Let's take up these issues in order to arrive at an answer that is best for you. There is no one answer for all individuals in regard to this question.

ARE YOU A FAIRLY INDEPENDENT TYPE OF PERSON?

I have frequently found that individuals who are very independent thinkers and traders often have difficulty with advisory services. They are prone to subscribe to a newsletter in order to determine whether the newsletter agrees with their own thinking. If they find there is agreement, then they use the newsletter as a further reason for making a trading decision based upon their own research. On the other hand, if the conclusion reached by the newsletter to which they subscribe is different from their own conclusion, they tend to minimize the importance of the letter, make their own trading decision, and discount the validity of the decision reached by the newsletter writer. In addition, individuals who are fairly independent should have no need for any type of newsletter since they should not really care about what any newsletter writer says. In fact, they shouldn't care about what anyone in the market says; whether they are a newsletter writer, an economist, a government official, or their broker. Therefore, if you are truly an independent individual who makes trading decisions based on your own observations and system, then you do not need a newsletter. Informational services such as charts, statistics, and computer data that do not render advice or interpretations may still be necessary. These, however, are not what I consider to be advisory in their role.

Please recognize the fact that if you consider yourself to be a truly independent trader, you will not be tempted by any newsletter or advisor; no matter how great their record may be and no matter how great their claims may be. I believe that there is a great deal to be said in favor of truly independent market analysts and I sincerely believe that most traders should strive to this end. Unfortunately, however, many individuals do not have the time to develop, maintain, and follow their own trading system. Therefore, they must become dependent upon an advisor or market analyst. They may also frequently become dependent upon the services of a money manager or broker who provides management services through power of attorney or limited power of attorney. Therefore, even if you consider yourself to be a fairly independent individual, your time constraint may require you to seek advisory services and you must, therefore, be willing to submit some of your independent attitudes and expectations to the advice of an advisor. This may be a difficult thing for you to do if you are prone toward great independence. I would rather see an independent individual not subscribe to a newsletter, spend only a limited amount of time on a trading system and investment approach, and make only a few investments and trades due to time constraint, than see an individual struggle with a newsletter, bucking its recommendations, or preselecting them, due to a personality conflict. If you consider yourself to be independent, then I suggest you stay that way and work out an approach that will satisfy your need for independence.

IF YOU DECIDE TO USE AN ADVISORY SERVICE

Here are some important things for you to remember in connection with the advisory service you have selected. It matters little what the service is or if your service deals exclusively with futures or stocks. There are some important rules that are applicable to advisory services, regardless of the particular newsletter you have actually selected.

Do Some Research Before You Decide

Before you decide which advisory service or services to choose, it is best to do a little research. You may think that obtaining a track record for each service is the primary consideration. I can tell you from personal experience in having reviewed many newsletters, that track records are not necessarily the single most consideration. As a matter of fact, track records can be quite misleading since many of them are based on hypothetical results. Even in cases where track records are based on actual trading results, there may be some inconsistencies with what may have actually transpired in the market and with the particular account that you may have traded according to the recommendation. Here are some items to consider when you do your investigating:

1. How much capital was required to make the recommended trades?

2. Have commission costs been deducted from the profit figure?

3. Are price of entry and price of exit based on figures which could have been achieved or are they hypothetical?

4. For how long, on the average, was each position held?

5. Were the positions established in multiples or in single units?

6. What was the maximum draw down in the hypothetical account?

7. In other words, how far against you could the account or systems have moved before returning in your favor?

8. How large of a stop loss order might have been required on the average?

9. How much was the average loss and how much was the average profit?

10. How consistent was performance throughout the years?

11. How many losing trades in a row did the system or newsletter make?

12. Are the recommendations of the service specific? Some services hedge their recommendations so that they are never totally wrong.

13. Attempt to determine if the service makes specific recommendations at specific prices with specific exit levels.

14. Is the service orientated toward intermediate term, long term, or short term?

15. Is the orientation specific to your needs?

16. How many subscribers does the service have? Although it is not usually possible to obtain precise figures on the number of subscribers for a service, it is very possible to arrive at a general estimate regarding the popularity and readership of the service. This can usually be done by examining the amount of advertising done by a service. Generally

speaking, the more a service advertises, the more subscribers it will have. It has usually been my impression that once an advisory service gets too big, there is a concomitant decrease in the quality and profitability of the recommendations. I am not saying this is always the case. It is merely a personal observation. One thing, however, that is certain is that once a service becomes too large, its recommendations will most definitely have an effect on the markets. Historically, there have been many examples of this; however, I see no need to cite specific names.

17. Is the service published by a brokerage operation? Some advisory services are distributed by branch operations of brokerage houses. I think it is important for you to determine if there is a relationship between the newsletter, the newsletter writer, and a brokerage firm. The existence of such a connection is not necessarily a negative indication; however, I believe it is important for the investor to know that the newsletter may not be completely free from conflict of interest in regard to the number of recommendations that will be made and the length at which they will be held. After all, brokerage firms and brokers make money on commissions. I would only be concerned about this possible connection if trading was excessive or if positions were held for an exceptionally short period of time (i.e., several days). Another issue to consider is the fact that in many instances, brokerage houses are hired by corporations who seek to sell additional shares of stock in their company through a new offering or a secondary distribution. In issues of this nature, I would take some time to determine whether there is any relationship between the newsletter and the frequency of recommendations.

18. Who is the newsletter writer? Is the newsletter written by an individual or a team? How long has the individual or team been doing work? The reasons for asking these questions are merely to determine the level of experience of the newsletter writer(s) or advisor(s). Experience, in and of itself, does not necessarily correlate with good research.

However, certain types of experience do lend good support to successful research. Educational backgrounds in areas such as computer programming, mathematics, economics, psychology, engineering, or science appear to have a good correlation with successful research.

19. Does the advisor trade or invest on his or her own recommendations? There are two important considerations in regard to this issue. In fact, there are two school of thoughts. Only you can decide where you stand. Some individuals believe that an advisor should not trade for his or her own account since its likely to influence his or her judgment. On the other hand, some individuals believe that it is necessary and preferable for an advisor to trade since it will keep the advisor in touch with the markets.

13

Trading Systems, Advisory Services, and Your Behavior

Upon first examination, it may seem that one's selection of a trading system has virtually nothing to do with either one's personality, behavior, or attitudes. Most individuals believe that a trading system is the only variable that distinguishes market winners from market losers. I disagree. Trading systems are a "dime a dozen." Some are better than others and some are, in fact, terrible. Trading systems can easily be tested and verified on computer. Although such results are frequently ideal, the performance of any trading system in real time can be shored up to compensate for slippage factors which cannot be accounted for during computer testing. The fact remains, nevertheless, that it is a fairly objective task to evaluate a trading system. It may take time and money, but it can be done. There is no reason, therefore, for today's investors and speculators to be using trading systems which are inferior in their potential performance.

My point has repeatedly been that a trading system is not as important as is its implementation. I have also pointed out that implementation of a trading system is significantly affected by investor personality, temperament, attitude, and, primarily, learned behaviors.

The output of any trading system must, prior to implementation, be filtered through the perception of the trader. As you know, the perception of the trader can do strange things to the ultimate implementation of trading and timing signals. I have also found that attitude, behavior, and personality influence the trading systems the individual ultimately selects, or the lack of trading system that an individual ultimately selects. This is a very significant point: If personality does affect the selection of a trading system, then an individual, by virtue of choice, can either facilitate or complicate the road to success. For example, an individual could select a very simple trading system requiring limited amount of time, or could select a very complicated, time-consuming system. If the trading system which has been selected is far too complicated and time-consuming to implement, then there is the likelihood that it will not be followed consistently and that one will fall behind in one's "market homework." This would severely limit success. There are other possibilities in the selection process, many of which will be discussed in this chapter. Even if you have already selected a trading system which pleases you, you might consider some of the points raised in this chapter and reevaluate your selection based upon the points I have raised. Remember that the bottom line is performance. If your trading system is performing as expected and if you are pleased with your real time results, don't even bother with this evaluation. However, if you have been disappointed in your expectations or if you find that in theory your system works well, but in practice it fails to achieve results, then you may have selected a trading system which is not compatible with either your attitudes, behaviors, or temperament.

HOW ARE TRADING SYSTEMS AND ADVISORY SERVICES USUALLY SELECTED?

I have already discussed the importance of being systematic, operational, and sequential in your implementation of market entry and exit. I have also suggested that the benefits of following a specific trading system far outweigh the disadvantages. Even though decisions made on the basis of emotion can on occasion produce wonderful results, such results are not consistent, and therefore, not dependable. Trading systems, on the other hand, are more likely to be consistent and fairly regular in their performance over long periods of time. Furthermore, trading systems can be tested, verified, and evaluated on an ongoing basis in real time. Hunches, guesses, tips, rumors, and so on cannot be subjected to such in-depth analysis.

The usual method by which investors select a trading system or advisory service is by examining their "track record." If a track record looks impressive and shows that large profits are possible, then the investor feels that this particular system or service should be considered in making his or her choice. Unfortunately, this process of selection does not answer many of the important questions that have significant implications for the individual investor or trader. It is important to know, for example, how much work and time commitment are required in order to implement the system effectively. Many traders and investors cannot make the time commitment.

Trading systems may frequently suffer large capital drawdowns in the course of operation. It is important for the investor to know what the maximum drawdown has been for the given system, particularly if his or her total available capital is limited. In many instances, a good trading system will be given up as a losing system simply because it is going through a period during which it is giving back some of the capital that it has made.

Another point to consider is the total number of trades and the commission generated by those trades. When studying a performance record or track record it is important to consider how much commission was paid in order to generate the amount of potential profit being claimed. With this advent of competitive commission rates and discount brokers in the 1980s, it is very possible to attain good performance with systems that were once marginal since the total cost of commissions is decreased. How does the investor feel about active trading? How does the trader feel about relatively infrequent trading?

A consideration ordinarily not given sufficient attention is the precise daily schedule which will be required in order to follow a given system precisely. Assume, for example, that a system requires market entry and exit during the day. Assume also that the user of the system, due to constraints of his or her occupation, cannot be in touch with the markets on a consistent enough basis. Although a system looks very promising, it is necessary to consider one's ability, or lack thereof, to follow the system in accordance with its rules. Traders are often overwhelmed by the promise of great profits; therefore they fail to consider the pragmatic aspects of system implementation.

It is fairly evident from the foregoing that the "bottom line" of a trading system is not profit alone but practical application as well. There must be a good blend of profits and pragmatics. I maintain that the trader or investor who does not consider the above points, or who, in fact, does consider the above points but chooses to ignore them, is expressing an important aspect of his or her personality. I also think that certain trading systems attract certain types of investors, just as certain types of automobiles attract certain types of individuals. Do you want a fast car that's impractical and costly to operate but impressive; *or*, do you want a slow car that helps you save money and requires little care or operating expense? My purpose in the description of trading system selection has been to refresh your memory as to the rational and reasonable methods by which a trading system or advisory service should be selected.

WHO CHOOSES SYSTEMS BASED ON FUNDAMENTALS?

Is it reasonable to say that certain types of investors are attracted to systems which analyze fundamentals as opposed to systems that study nothing but technical factors? After studying investor personality and behavior for many years, I have come to the conclusion that this is indeed true! We all know, for example, that bankers, economists, farmers, as well as individuals in the manufacturing and food processing businesses are very closely tied to the laws of supply and demand. Ultimately, supply and demand are the basis of long-term price trends. Such individuals, by virtue of their occupation and education, are closely tied to supply and demand, as well as other fundamental considerations which comprise pricing structure. I have chosen to use the word "ultimately" since it is a fact that the laws of economics, in the long run, determine the price of most commodities. However, in the short run, and over the very near term, the fundamentals do not necessarily tell the whole story. There may be significant price movements, entirely contrary to what the ideal trend should be, based strictly upon the fundamentals. To ignore what transpires on the short term may very well be the appropriate thing to do. However, over the short run the investor may be forced to abandon a position due to the contrary nature of the short-term trend.

While long-term trends are ultimately based upon fundamentals, I contend that short-term trends are primarily based upon the perception and interpretation of technical factors. Technical market considerations are more useful on a short-term basis. Therefore, if one selects a trading system based entirely on fundamentals, one is expressing an aspect of personality. A strict adherence to fundamentals says that the individual is closely tied to underlying causes and requires cause and effect explanations, not only in his or her life, but in trading and investing as well.

Such an approach is not without its benefits. Jack Schwager (1983) made the following cogent points in his study of fundamentals:

> The cause-and-effect relationship is entirely the province of fundamental analysis. In contrast, intrinsically all methods of technical analysis are based on patterns. Thus, the trader who wishes to understand a market's behavior must turn to fundamental analysis. Some of the key attributes of fundamental analysis include the following:
>
> 1. Fundamental analysis provides an extra dimension of information not available to the purely technical trader.
>
> 2. Fundamentals may sometimes portend a major price move well in advance of any technical signals.

3. A knowledge of fundamentals would permit a trader to adopt a more aggressive stance in those situations in which the fundamentals suggest the potential for a major price move.

4. An understanding of the underlying fundamentals can provide the incentive to stay with a winning trade.

5. The way in which a market responds to fundamental news can be used as a trading tool—even by the technical trader.

Unfortunately, much of the conventional wisdom about fundamental analysis is inaccurate.*

Of the points listed by Schwager, 3 and 4 are essentially psychological factors. Point 1 is informational, as is point 5. Point 2 can be claimed as an advantage by virtually any system or approach and is often a function of "20/20 hindsight." Therefore, psychological factors comprise a good portion of what Schwager lists as some of fundamental analysis' key attributes. Schwager's work is most excellent as well as revealing. To me it suggests that the "cause and effect" aspect of fundamental analysis is its main attraction to traders. This supports my claim that those who are avowed fundamentalists require reasons, explanations, cause and effect justification, and rational support for behavior, both in humans and in the markets. It is a known fact, however, that the reasons are not always relevant, logical, or observable.

Therefore, staunch fundamentalists may not understand many of the short-term fluctuations that occur within secular trends. By being tied to nothing but what is clearly observable, such individuals can be setting themselves up for frustration and failure. They are ignoring potentially important technical and psychological market factors. Their performance and relationships with the markets could be significantly improved if they added a dimension of the "unseen" or illogical to their investment decisions and selections. What I am saying is that *strict adherence to a system which analyzes only fundamental factors is a form of rigidity which can present a significant problem to the investor.* Therefore, the fervent proponent of strict fundamental analysis (to the exclusion of other factors) is too tied to cause and effect. This intensely rigid

*Schwager, Jack D. *A Complete Guide to the Futures Markets.* Wiley, New York, 1984, p. 18.

focus could, in the long run, prove destructive. Fundamentalists would do well to read chapters 1–11 of Schwager's book.

THE PURELY TECHNICAL APPROACH

On the other end of the continuum, and therefore also an extremist position, is the purely technical approach. The individual who is attracted to such a technique is also to a great extent expressing a form of rigid personality. This individual, however, is less likely to be trapped by rigidity, since technical conditions in the marketplace are very sensitive to price change. An overwhelming majority of technical signals are determined as a function of price. In other words, almost every technical trading system will be responsive to price. *Price, however, is not always responsive to fundamentals.* I urge you to consider this last statement very seriously since it clearly explains why I believe that the pure technician is in a more advantageous position than is the pure fundamentalist. I repeat what I just said. Most technical trading systems derive their signals from such factors as chart formations (created by price) derivations of price, volume, open interest, and so on. These are all related to price trend. In other words, 99% of all so called technical analysis is based on either anticipating change in trend or in following change in trend. Such change in trend is measured by analyzing derivations of price related data. Technical approaches follow price and price follows supply and demand.

There are literally thousands, or even hundreds of thousands of examples in which fundamental factors failed to affect price. One could argue that the fundamentals commonly known to the public are not necessarily the fundamentals which affect price, and that, therefore, were they known, we could clearly see that fundamentals did, in fact, play a role in price trend. This is, however, a moot point since a majority of the "secret fundamentals" are not known to the public and therefore not useful for speculation or investing. Technical price formations or technical factors in the market are, however, very responsive to price change, and therefore, quick to respond to changes in the market. Individuals who select totally technical/mechanical trading systems based on price derivation are in an advantageous position. Should their "investments" move against them, they will probably be out of their positions more quickly than will individuals whose trades are based entirely upon fundamentals. Therefore, losses are ideally taken more quickly and, provided the system is followed, the losses are not as large as they might be from a fundamentally based trading system.

In spite of the fact that selection of a totally mechanical, totally technical trading system may seem to be somewhat radical and close-minded, you can see that there is some good justification for doing so (if my reasoning is correct). I conclude that the individual who is totally committed to a mechanical/technical trading system is in good touch with the actual nature of market movement. The individual is most likely not as interested in long-term moves as is the fundamentalist. There, are, nevertheless, some fairly good and successful long-term oriented technical systems. This further supports the notion that whether for long-term or short-term objectives, mechanical/technical trading systems are preferable to fundamentally based trading systems.

I realize that I may arouse the wrath of fundamentalists throughout the world by taking this position; however, I believe that technical analysis is a logical outgrowth of the behavioral approach to understanding human behavior. This is not to say that technicians are always logical! As an example, I could cite a hypothetical situation whereby a technical trading system signaled a short sale in a futures market. At the same time very bullish news was released causing the market to "lock" limit up. The technical trader who was being rational and reasonable, might be dissuaded from taking a short position immediately, bowing to "good sense" and the expectation that prices will go even higher the next day. The technical trader whose personality might be too rigid would probably take a position regardless of this news, and might, in fact, take a large loss as a result. Although there is much to be said for consistency and strict adherence to the rules, (whether technican or fundamentalists) the individual who is rigidly tied to following all rules, even in the face of almost certain information to the contrary, is likely to be expressing a basic personality flaw. Therefore, individuals who select extreme types of trading systems should question the validity of their choice.

EXTREMELY INTRICATE/COMPLICATED TRADING SYSTEMS

I once heard a joke that appropriately describes how I feel about the selection of a trading system which is extremely intricate and excessively complex. I know that it is now possible, with the assistance of computer technology, to have a system or a method of analysis that is extremely complicated mathematically, compared to what was possible not too many years ago. I do not include in the category of "extremely complicated," trading systems all based on computer methods; rather, my comments are directed at trading systems which are either too intricate in their implementation or so mathematically complex that even the computer seems to have difficulty generating the output consistently and/or promptly. I think this will become more clear to you after I tell you my little joke.

It seems a young man was driving his sports car on the highway one day. While doing so, he happened to notice a chicken running behind his automobile. Somewhat surprised, he glanced at his speedometer and realized that the chicken was running at a fairly good rate of speed. This intrigued him, so he increased his speed to approximately 60 miles per hour. He observed that the chicken, undaunted, was still in pursuit. Good sense gave way to curiosity and the gentleman increased his speed to about 100 miles per hour. Unaffected by this breakneck speed, the chicken persisted. After a lengthy chase at high speeds, the chicken abruptly made his exit from the highway, and in so doing sped by the fast moving vehicle, taking the lead in this strange race.

When the chicken sped by, the motorist began to pursue at even higher speed. He became obsessed (you might say "driven") with the notion of determining what made the chicken run so fast. The chase led to a large chicken farm on the outskirts of a town. Suddenly, in a cloud of feathers and dust, the chicken disappeared into a maze of chicken coops and hen houses. The motorist proceeded to park his car at what appeared to be the main building. He entered. Sitting inside were a farmer, the farmer's wife, and what seemed to be the farmer's son. In his frustration, the motorist exclaimed, "That's the fastest chicken I ever saw!" The farmer replied, in a matter of fact tone, "Yep, they sure are fast, aren't they?" "What makes them so darned fast?" inquired the bewildered motorist. "Well, I've been developing this breed of chicken for the last 25 years. I've spent millions in genetic research and I have finally succeeded in breeding a three-legged chicken. . . . That's right, these chickens have three legs!" explained the farmer. "Why three legs?" inquired the incredulous pursuer. "Well, there's just me, my wife, and my son in this here family, and we all like drumsticks. I figured there must be thousands of families throughout the world like us. There's no reason to kill two chickens to get four drumsticks, when you can kill one chicken and get three drumsticks, making everyone happy," replied the farmer. Obviously impressed with the tremendous research that went into developing the three-legged variety of chicken, the motorist asked, "Do they taste any different than normal chicken?" The farmer gave this last question considerable thought, apparently having come to some insight and realization as a result of the inquiry. After several minutes of thought he replied, "Don't rightly know so . . . they're so darned fast, I've never been able to catch one!"

I hope you find the point of this witticism quite clear. Many traders and investors devote hundreds of hours and thousands of dollars to intensive research and complicated trading systems that are so burdensome, so cumbersome, and so difficult to implement that they cannot, "ever catch them." You've probably known individuals like this. They seem to be very academic, extremely interested in fine details and fine tuning. In the process, they ignore pragmatics. An individual who is attracted to such trading systems, or one who develops such a trading system, is most likely employing an old psychological defense called "avoidance." By concentrating so intensely on a system and its perfection, one avoids dealing with the reality of the markets. Before you spend too much time, money, and energy on developing a complicated and burdensome trading system, ask yourself whether you have gone too far. In the market, simplicity is best.

THE "ULTIMATE" TRADING SYSTEM

For many years now, "ultimate" trading systems have been very popular items. They have sold well to a public constantly seeking perfections in the marketplace. The ultimate trading system has been packaged, sold, resold, repackaged, and sold again under many different names and to many different investors. This has been especially true in the futures markets, where rarely a month passes without a new and "astonishing" trading system making the rounds. Some individuals are repeatedly attracted to ultimate systems and pay large sums of money to purchase them. We are all entitled to be victims of pandering at least once or twice in the course of our lives. However, individuals who are attracted to the lure of such systems, repeatedly paying large sums of money to purchase them, deserve exactly what they get.

Many trading systems are very good ones indeed. They provide an objective, specific, and mechanical method for market entry and exit. Some trading systems are actually quite profitable in their hypothetical performance. All an individual really needs is one trading system that works well. Many people search for better and better trading systems in the same way medical researchers continue to search for better cures. The only difference is that medical research has virtually unlimited funds at disposal. This is not true of the investor. I maintain that virtually any trading system can be profitable provided it is consistently and diligently applied. Therefore, the never ending search for the perfect system is an illusion, a dream, a fantasy, and a waste of time. The individual who is constantly on the search for such a system or the individual who is constantly striving for perfection in one's own trading system, is telling us something about his or her personality. In effect, these individuals are saying that they do not have confidence in what they are now doing; they believe in the "magic" of an "ultimate trading system." By believing that one's trading system is not perfect, one can blame the system for losses, thereby avoiding taking personal responsibility. Furthermore, the never-ending search leaves the trader in a constant state of confusion and with an excuse to avoid establishing a solid, constant, and ongoing trading program. The repeated starting and stopping of different trading systems is bound to confuse, disorient, and, in the long run, frustrate.

If you are an individual searching for the "holy grail," and if you believe you have found the holy grail a number of times over, only to discover you still have found nothing, then you should ask yourself if your search is real or whether it is nothing more than a psychological game. The search for the perfect trading system is like the search for the pot of gold at the end of the rainbow. A person can waste an entire lifetime searching for the perfect trading system and it will never be found. Therefore, if your search for the perfect trading system has led you to nothing but expense, frustration, and disappointment ask yourself, "Why do I keep doing this?" The answers may be painful to accept, but it is a fact that your selection of trading systems reveals your personality.

PEOPLE DON'T ALWAYS CHOOSE WHAT'S BEST FOR THEM

Life would be simple indeed if people made choices based on what they really needed as opposed to what they wanted. Frequently, choices are made on what is truly necessary; however, much more often choices in life are made based upon the fulfillment of emotional and physical needs that may not necessarily be consistent with the psychological, spiritual, social, and intellectual advancement of the individual. We see this all around us. Any individual who would choose to become heavily involved with liquor, drugs, tobacco, religious cults, and so on, is an individual who has made a choice based upon wants rather than true needs. I have found that individuals are frequently attracted to trading systems, specific investments, brokerage firms, and trading systems as a result of some fantasy, distorted image, unrealistic expectation, or advertising ploy as opposed to logical reason which takes into consideration the many variables of a given situation. You must come to terms with your underlying motivation. Determine what lies under the surface of your decision. Frequently, motivation is not as clear as it should be. Even though many of our friends and family may clearly see our motivation, we ourselves are not aware of it. Some of the questionnaires provided in this book will help you recognize your motivation. In so doing, you will make more informed choices about the markets.

You should also remember that there is a close connection between what you tell yourself and what you actually believe. If you tell yourself something long enough, you will eventually begin to believe it. Assume that you have purchased a trading system and after several months you begin to realize that it does not work as well as it should. You know you have done everything right in following the system's instructions and rules. However, the system just does not work. You have two choices. You can either cut your losses short and get rid of the system, or you can begin to tell yourself that the system will work, "it just needs more time." If the system continues to fail, you have the opportunity for similar choices along the way. At each point you may ask yourself the same question. "Does the system work?" Obviously if it doesn't work, it doesn't work, and you should get rid of it. If, however, the system doesn't work and you find you are saying, "It needs more time; I know it will work; it has to work; it was very expensive; so and so said it was a great system; the track record looks great . . ." or any number of other self-deceptions, then you are simply rationalizing, and you soon will actually begin to believe that all the things you are telling yourself are true. Therefore, remember, *it is important to be honest with others, but it is more important to be honest with yourself.*

MAGIC, SECRET NUMBERS, ASTROLOGY, AND OTHERS

There are probably as many trading systems as there are people. Way back in the 1920s, Burton Pugh published *The Science and Secrets of Wheat Trading**. In his series of very thin booklets, Pugh

*Pugh, Burton. *The Science and Secrets of Wheat Trading*. Lambert Gann: Pomeroy, Wash., 1978, orig. 1933. Book 5, p. 10.

disclosed his secret trading system for wheat, and explained, therein, his success in the wheat market. His reasons were quite simple, as was his trading system. I, myself, cannot do the explanation justice. Therefore, I quote from Pugh:

> Not one trader in a hundred thinks of the moon in making his deals or even notices what phase is in force. It is the general optimism that is in him, or the pessimism, engendered by outside forces and often his inspiration comes from the old, almost submerged, ancient moon complex that harks back to his ancestral days.

> Thus the moon effects are mild. They are gently, almost imperceptibly persuasive. The phases gain their power by widespread effect since they touch men in all lands and thus mildly affect world markets. They are so mild that they lose their effect during times of sudden or great stress. A declaration of war between two great nations or a killing hot wave or withering dust storm over wheat countries will completely upset the harmony of the market with the phases FOR A TIME. [1933, Book 5, p. 10]

> Astonishingly soon the options will fall in line with the phases again or will show enough obedience to them to the extent that they can be used to great advantage. The author again warns the student that, fascinating as this moon effect is, it has serious variations and must be used observingly. In the pages which follow every important variation is shown and the reason given why. Then the student is shown the styles of market action in which the two phases deliver their maximum effect and how they may be used to the greatest advantage.

> The author of this course uses the phases unceasingly. At times they afford no help. At other times they form the only means by which an important move can be forecasted. The moon is not an independent method of forecasting movements but is of high value in locating the turning points.

Figure 13.1 shows a graphic example of Pugh's trading system. Through the years, I have seen many such trading systems. You can see from the illustration that Pugh's technique consisted of buying on the full moon and selling on the new moon. One might conclude from his work that some sort of lunar affect was at the base of these movements in the price of wheat. While it may very well be true that this is the case, my interest is not in determining *why* something works, but rather, *whether* it works.

Therefore, my conclusion about all of the trading systems and

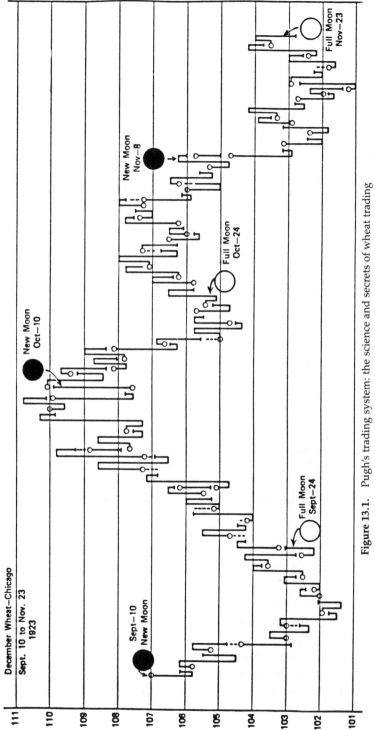

Figure 13.1. Pugh's trading system: the science and secrets of wheat trading

analytical methods that are based upon indicators not commonly considered rational or reasonable by the investing community is that we should give every technique a fair chance to perform. I prefer not be judgmental until I know the facts. In all truthfulness, I have seen individuals achieve amazing results using some of the simplest trading systems available.

Not too many years ago, an elderly gentleman came up to speak with me following a speech I had just made to a group of Alabama producers. He offered to teach me his "trading system." Suddenly he produced, seemingly out of nowhere, a chart book and a string from which was suspended a small metal sphere. Before I could react he was holding the ball and string above the chart. Then, with the string in one hand he steadied the ball carefully so that there was virtually no movement. Suddenly the ball started to move again, but only by the slightest, almost imperceptable amount. Perhaps it was some tension left in the string that made the ball move. I honestly don't know what caused it to move, but causes are really of no consequence. "There we go," he exclaimed. "Looks like it is time to buy hog futures." Perhaps I should have been taken aback by this revelation, yet I took it in stride. I tried to be logical about what I saw. Also, I felt very kindly toward the elderly gentleman, and seeing the gleam of excitement and belief in his eyes, I hadn't the heart to ridicule or criticize his "trading system." Logically I asked him the following questions. "What are the details of your trading system?" "First," he replied, "North-South movement means 'buy' . . . East-West means 'sell.' Second, if I take up a position in the market using my timing indicator here, and if that position show a loss by the end of the day, I close the sucker out!," he exclaimed. "In other words, you keep what shows you a profit by the end of the day, and you get rid of what shows you a loss at the end of the day. Is that correct?," I inquired. "Hell, yes!. . . .A fella would have to be a darned fool to keep a losing position overnight, no matter how good his trading system is."

Here, in a small southern town, miles from my home, I experienced first hand one of the most important principles of successful trading systems. The basis of most successful trading is so simple that virtually any investor or trader can learn it. This principle is clearly and specifically, *"cut your losses and let your profits run."* Almost every trading system has the potential to be a winning trading system as long as this and several other rules are followed religiously. The "divining rod" system used by this elderly gentleman was merely a trading system based upon random selection of trades with consistent application of money management techniques.

Even after all of my many years of study with trading systems I would have to say that a trading system without the application of strict money management techniques is a useless trading system. A trading system which seems to be useless may, in effect, be made profitable with the application of money management principles. Therefore, when you analyze a system make certain that you do not accept it or reject it strictly on the basis of its underlying rational or trade selection principles. Always consider the money management principles that accompany it whether the system is based on the stars, the moon, the planets, extra-sensory perception, or for that matter any other seemingly peculiar justification or approach. In trading and investing it is the bottom line that counts. Those who pick such systems should not be judged too harshly or prematurely! It is their performance that counts!

14

Evaluating Your Attitude, Opinions, and Responses

Market technicians will tell you that the most important part of any trading system is the manner in which it evaluates market conditions and then generates signals to buy, sell, or hold. In other words, a trading system takes inventory of certain indicators and then, based on a predetermined configuration of these indicators, lets the user know how to approach the market. In other words, there are two steps. They are (1) *evaluation* and (2) *action*.

These two elements are crucial to the trading and investing process. A third aspect is *ongoing evaluation*, but this is part of any ongoing system. The same sequence of actions holds true in the evaluation of your trading attitudes, behaviors, and results. The first step is to evaluate what you have been doing. The second step is to change what you don't like. For all too many years people have taken what I consider to be the wrong approach to improving investor performance. The prevailing opinion has been that if a trader is not successful, then it must surely be the system he or she is using. As you know, I have spent many chapters illustrating why I believe that this is not entirely true. The important thing is first to *evaluate* yourself, and then to *change* yourself. The person most likely to succeed in this process is *you*. Many people might disagree with me. "How can you be objective about yourself?" they might ask. Their queries are well-founded. In response, I say that if you have the right tools and methods of self-evaluation, and if you have the assistance of another party in the process, (a close friend, spouse, etc.) then you are very likely to succeed.

Third, it is important to continue the evaluation process even after changes and improvements have been made. As in the case of a trading system, ongoing evaluation and follow-up of your "position" is necessary. This includes your personal "position" relative to the markets. Therefore, one must always remember that growth and development of trading skills are one-half of the equation. One must also remember that ongoing growth can be realized by continued evaluation.

This chapter deals with evaluating your behavior in the markets as a prerequisite to changing your behavior. We will begin with the premise that you are not pleased with your market performance. The next step is, of course, to evaluate yourself to see if there are other areas of your investment behavior that warrant change or, at the very minimum, close observation. As a way of determining where you stand, a simple list of questions should be answered and you will then score yourself. This questionnaire seeks to obtain a global picture of your attitudes and behaviors in order to highlight any possible weak points of which you may not be aware. The forerunner of this questionnaire appeared in *The Investor's Quotient* (Wiley, 1980). For this text, the questions have been refined, reevaluated, and expanded. More questions have been added, and the answer key has been made more specific in order to suggest possible methods by which behavior might be changed.

The questionnaire contained in this chapter is not intended to serve as a scientific psychiatric evaluation that has been researched in accordance with the necessary methods and procedures customary in psychological testing. It is *not* a psychological test. The questionnaire seeks merely to evaluate in a general way your attitudes, responses, and expectations in trading. It seeks to highlight areas of strength and areas of weakness based on the principles which have been explained in this book. These principles were derived from my understanding of trader and investor behavior, my work and my interviews with traders and investors, and my observations of errors most frequently made by investors and speculators.

Since the questionnaire is not a strict scientific technique, it cannot answer all questions, nor can it pinpoint all areas of problematic behavior or potential problematic behavior. However, as a general guideline it should be used as follows: (1) Fill out the evaluation honestly, completely, and above all, slowly. Take some time to think about each of the questions. Do not attempt to "figure out" the right answer, however, be more concerned about your answer. The right answer is your answer. Even if your answer is the wrong answer, it is still the right answer. I am not seeking to determine how smart you are or how well you are doing in the markets; I seek to help you determine if and why there are reasons that you may not be achieving all you can in the markets. (2) Take time and go through the answer key provided at the end of this chapter. In particular, pay close attention to those answers which are not consistent with what I have indicated as the "preferred answers." I have given sufficient leeway in scoring to allow some disagreement with my preferred answers. In other words you do not need a "perfect score" to rate high in "your investor's quotient." (3) Take notes and refer to various sections in the text that explain methods of overcoming problems that may be related to the particular question or questions for which you failed to give the preferred response. (4) Use this questionnaire as a guideline for setting up a specific program by which you plan to overcome your limitations as highlighted by your responses. In particular, if you score especially low, make certain you have a program or schedule and that you do so as soon as possible.

Another thing you should consider is a regular reading program of books written by the "great traders." Some of these books are listed in the bibliography at the end of this book.

You must remember that the process of correcting market behaviors that are either unprofitable, unacceptable, or inappropriate is an individual matter. It is impossible for any one book or any one methodology to change or rectify the trading profile of all traders. It takes time, persistence, and great motivation to put the right answers into operation. I have observed that, in most cases, individuals are well acquainted with the solutions of their problems. The solutions themselves are quite simple. It is, however, the application of these solutions that one finds difficult. We all know that the "cure" for most forms of overweight is diet. However, the tens of millions who are suffering from overweight conditions are not suffering from lack of knowledge, they are suffering from lack of ability. We know the answers to overcoming the negative effects of drinking and smoking. However, many of us cannot put the solutions into action. The same is true of investor behavior. We know that preparation, consistency, perseverance, motivation, and so on are the solutions. However, we do not know how to put these solutions into action. Although the questionnaire in this chapter will help us to find the problem areas as well as the solutions, this chapter, this book, this author, or for that matter, any power cannot put the solutions into action unless the investor takes the first step and the initiative in making the solution a reality.

At some point in the future, after you have set your programs into action, complete this questionnaire again. See how your attitudes and behaviors may have changed. Again, be honest with yourself in answering the questions and provide answers which truthfully describe what you feel and believe. Score yourself again. See how you've changed, and see if the change has been for the positive. If change has indeed been in the area of a significantly high overall score, then chances are that your profits have also increased or, at the very minimum, your losses have begun to diminish.

Trader Evaluation Profile

1. I trade primarily for the short term.
2. I rarely use stop loss orders: "mental" or otherwise.

3. A broker's job is to provide his customers with good trades.

4. I often spend sleepless nights worrying about the markets.

5. I tend to ignore "news" good or bad: my trading system anticipates news.

6. My behavior at home is "intolerable" if I've lost money in the market.

7. Brokers make you lose money by getting you in and out of the market too often.

8. I often worry about losses long after they have been taken.

9. Most of my profits have come from following my trading system as closely as possible.

10. I am beginning to believe that I will never be a winner in the markets.

11. I have a set time for working on my market studies each day or week.

12. In order to trade successfully it is necessary to gather as much market information as possible.

13. The markets are "fixed" to help "insiders": take money away from the public.

14. My broker gets me out of profitable trades too soon.

15. I do not allow any other opinions to influence me.

16. I subscribe to more than six advisory services.

17. My positions are often closed out before I have timing signals to do so.

18. I have a full time job other than the market but call for price quotes during the day.

19. I close out trades only when my system dictates so.

20. I prefer to buy on strength and sell on weakness.

21. Making money in the commodity and stock markets is just a form of business and requires patience plus experience.

22. Trading with the trend is the best way to make money.

23. I have accounts at several different brokerage houses so that I can get the opinions of several different experts.

24. Day trading is best done by those who are in constant touch with the markets.

25. I change trading systems quite often.

26. My average losing trade is larger than my average profitable trade.

27. When I don't feel just right I cut down on the amount of trading I do. Sometimes I don't trade at all.

28. I alone am fully responsible for my profits and losses.

29. The successful trader is one who tends to isolate himself or herself from others' opinions as much as possible (other than to place orders).

30. I have read the writings of such famous speculators as Gann, Livermore, Pugh, and Baruch.

31. I frequently get very frustrated about the market.

32. My largest single loss was the result of not following my trading system to the letter.

33. Emotion is the chief enemy of successful speculation if not controlled.

34. My trades are planned before or after market hours.

35. I frequently change my method of selecting grades.

36. I prefer not to have a specific trading system.

37. A 30% return per year on my commodity trading is highly acceptable.

38. Organization is one of the keys to success in the market. Although it is possible to succeed without being organized, the chances are better if one has a structured program to follow.

39. Most of the traders who lose money trading commodities do not have the necessary "inside information" necessary to make profits.

40. I feel such a great need to trade that I will not take vacations for fear of missing a move.

41. People say that I am very methodical in my approach to trading.

42. Once I have determined the direction of the next move I sit and patiently wait for the timing signal.

43. After several losses I begin to lose faith in my trading system.

44. My market studies (i.e., charting) tend to fall behind rather often.

45. I believe that I can learn how to trade the market profitably and with consistency.

46. My first trading decision is usually my best—when I change my mind, thereafter, I am usually wrong.

47. Many times I make trades in the market based on "gut feelings" or spur-of-the-moment decisions.

48. Most trading systems can make money if money management principles are used.

49. I frequently take larger than expected losses because I cannot accept the loss when it is within reason, taking it as prescribed by my trading system.

50. Losses cause me to experience prolonged periods of depression, self-pity, and/or sadness, which also affect my working situation.

ANSWER KEY

1. *Preferred Answer = No:*   Long-term trades are more indicative of successful trading psychology. Unless you trade the market as your only occupation, short-term day trades (scalps) are not an effective way to make profits on a consistent basis. This type of trading usually requires constant attention and is not typically an effective way for "the public" to make and keep money. Although some traders are very successful at this, most are not. Let the "floor traders" and professionals "day-trade." They know how to do it well. You can also do it well, but it requires full time attention, and you must learn how to do it.

2. *Preferred Answer = No:*   Not using stops can lead to far greater losses than expected. It is indicative of poor self-

discipline and generally ineffective trading technique. Fear of stops getting "picked" is understandable in very "thin" or inactive markets; in such instances, "mental stops" can help. In most markets, however, a well placed stop is more important than the "fear of being picked" that it may create. Limiting losses is one of the "keys" to success and should be incorporated in every trading system.

3. *Preferred Answer = No:* It is best to not depend on anyone's advice other than your own market studies. Brokers should be depended upon to provide good fills promptly rather than "good" trades. If you do intend to follow a broker's advice, then make certain you do so consistently. Only in so doing will you know how good his or her advice really is. If you "second guess" your broker or do not do as he or she says, then you will be using an incomplete trading strategy. You might be better off learning to do your own research, depending entirely on your own work for trading signals.

4. *Preferred Answer = No:* If you frequently lose sleep worrying about your positions in the market, this is a warning sign. You are most likely unsure of yourself, your system, and your trading in general. Possibly you are riding losses beyond the appropriate point, or perhaps, you are overtrading. Examine your overall trading very carefully and pay attention to this "early warning sign." Refer to some of the suggestions at the end of this report for possible assistance. Loss of sleep is a common symptom of anxiety. Anxiety indicates that there is something wrong internally.

5. *Preferred Answer = Yes:* Your answer indicated that you are confident enough to ignore "news" and its possible effect on the market. You realize that your trading system is best for you and you refuse to be swayed by momentary influences which create emotional highs and lows in price. This is a quality associated with market winners.

6. *Preferred Answer = No:* This is another warning signal. If you respond to market loss with "intolerable" home behav-

ior then you may be heading for trouble. Pay attention to this symptom. It is not part of an overall winning market psychology and signals trouble ahead. You may want to take a small vacation and examine your relationship to the markets.

7. *Preferred Answer = No:*   You must learn that you alone are responsible for your own actions. No person can "make" you do anything. To have such a belief or attitude suggests an immature or disorganized approach to trading and is another sign of poor market psychology.

8. *Preferred Answer = No:*   To worry incessantly about a loss after it has been taken is not indicative of good trading psychology. If you take a loss and understand why it was taken, then your lesson has been learned. Worrying about a loss or not understanding why it was taken can lead to further losses. This is not a success yielding response.

9. *Preferred Answer = Yes:*   Congratulations! This is one of the most effective indicators of good trading. Stay with your technique. It should continue to serve you well.

10. *Preferred Answer = No:*   Your response is indicative of a negative mental attitude. You may be "setting yourself up" to lose by admitting defeat. This is another danger sign and must be taken care of immediately.

11. *Preferred Answer = Yes:*   Good. This is an effective market skill and should be continued. It is an indicator of maturity and winning trader psychology. Continue with the good work. If you have this skill but still do not show net profits, then continue with this evaluation. Some answers may be found in the summary of suggestions at the bottom of this evaluation.

12. *Preferred Answer = No:*   Information is not as important as how it is used or who is using it. It is not only necessary to have information. It is necessary to use the information. Information alone will not guarantee success. Implementation of information on a consistent basis will help make success more probable.

13. *Preferred Answer = No:*   You may wish to examine your attitudes. Although it is true that markets are manipulated from time to time, "insiders" are not preventing the public from making money. You have most likely had some bad experiences in the market. This has turned you against those who can trade profitably. You may want to change your beliefs, if possible, since they will not help you profit in their current state.

14. *Preferred Answer = No:*   You alone are in control. Until you realize this, you will not have the success you seek. See Item 7.

15. *Preferred Answer = Yes:*   Your trading system is best for you. And you have come to clearly appreciate the value of listening only to your own research. This is an attitude which should bring success in the market.

16. *Preferred Answer = No:*   Too much information is not healthy. You are either insecure about your trading system, or perhaps, you do not have one. You might be better off subscribing to only one service and following all of its recommendations religiously. Be careful about getting too much information. It is most often a sign of insecurity.

17. *Preferred Answer = No:*   The fact that your trades are closed out prior to hitting their objectives is indicative of poor trading technique. Either you are being scared out, or you are not following your plans. If your trades are being stopped out at the predetermined loss point, then you are following the trading program. Examine your trading rules and discipline if your trades are closed out prior to objectives, particularly if those objectives are hit after you get out.

18. *Preferred Answer = No:*   Full-time employment other than the market is not consistent with short-term trading. Moreover, calling for quotes many times each day is a sign of uncertainty and insecurity. Even if you trade for the long term you should train yourself to be more secure. Try not to call for price quotes too often. You may be prompted to

act prematurely and you may also be alienating your broker.

19. *Preferred Answer = Yes:* Your answer indicates that you have the self-discipline which is necessary in profitable trading. You are confident enough about your system to liquidate trades at the proper times. You score one point in the area of effective market psychology.

20. *Preferred Answer = Yes:* Although it is hard to do, buying on strength and selling on weakness is a profitable procedure in most markets. Trading with the trend is the sign of a successful or potentially successful trader. This is a good quality.

21. *Preferred Answer = Yes:* Correct. The market should be treated as a form of business. It can be used to make money if, and only if, the proper rules of effective management are followed. You recognize this fact and this is an asset in profitable market psychology.

22. *Preferred Answer = Yes:* Although this is obvious, trading with the trend is the best way to make and keep money in most markets. Certainly there are times when "whipsaw" markets will get you in and out frequently. But for the most part, trend trading brings large profits. If you have the ability to trade with the trend, maintain it and elaborate on it. If you are lacking in this skill, then you must concentrate on acquiring it. (See also Item 20.)

23. *Preferred Answer = No:* This is not a good strategy to follow. It is preferable to trade only on your own information. There's nothing wrong with having several accounts at different houses. This should not be done with the intention of getting "expert information." If having several different accounts serves a good purpose other than obtaining information, then there is nothing wrong with it.

24. *Preferred Answer = Yes:* Those who day trade or "scalp" the markets should be in touch with prices at all times of the day. If you do not realize that this is the case, then you may be in for some painful surprises.

25. *Preferred Answer = No:*   Before deciding you need a new trading system make certain you are using your current system correctly. In fact, make certain you are using a system. Many traders are not employing a specific technique and don't realize it.

26. *Preferred Answer = No:*   The bottom line is that you are a net loser. This is most likely due to your own shortcomings rather than those of your system. Make certain that your ideal system results are virtually the same as your actual results. If this is so, then your system is at fault. If not, then you are at fault.

27. *Preferred Answer = Yes:*   It is good to cut down on your trading when you don't feel right. The market won't run away. Not trading when you feel bad is a sign of maturity.

28. *Preferred Answer = Yes:*   This is a very mature response. Personal responsibility for all profits and losses is a winning attitude.

29. *Preferred Answer = Yes:*   Your answer indicates an understanding of how important it is to keep away from external influences. This is a winning attitude.

30. *Preferred Answer = Yes:*   The well-rounded trader has read the classics. They will be very helpful in the long run. Your readings should be pursued.

31. *Preferred Answer = No:*   The market should not cause you frequent frustration. It is normal to become aggravated every now and then. But if you are getting upset more than once a month, you may have developed poor trading attitudes.

32. *Preferred Answer = No:*   You have not followed your system and the market has let you know about it in no uncertain terms. If this is still happening, then you could get into much more serious difficulty. Either learn to follow the system or stop trading for a while!

33. *Preferred Answer = Yes:*   Your recognition of this fact is a positive indication. Emotion can be used as an indicator of

when others are making market errors. As long as you control your own emotions you will fare well.

34. *Preferred Answer = Yes:* The fact that you plan trades before or after market hours is a sign of effective organization and a winning methodical approach. Those who make decisions about positions during market hours (unless short-term trading is their profession) are bound to make many irrational decisions.

35. *Preferred Answer = No:* Frequent changes in trading systems are generally indicative of insecurity and poor trading psychology. More often than not, it is the trader and not the system which is at fault. Your "yes answer" suggests that you may need to improve your self-confidence and positive attitudes.

36. *Preferred Answer = No:* Lack of specific trading system is often detrimental. There are some individuals who have the mental and intellectual capacity to function successfully without a detailed method of trade selection—but they are in the minority. Your results might be improved if you committed your technique to paper using precise rules.

37. *Preferred Answer = Yes:* Your willingness to be satisfied with a 30% return is indicative of a positive attitude. It also suggests lack of greed and a mature approach to profit making. You still maintain a positive attitude by indicating that anything over 30% will make you even happier.

38. *Preferred Answer = Yes:* Your realization that organized traders fare better suggests a winning market attitude. Make certain that your opinion is backed up by action. Only in so doing will you benefit from the proper attitude.

39. *Preferred Answer = No:* It is not necessary to have "inside information" in order to be successful. If you believe that only those who lack such information are losers, then you may be suffering from feelings of suspiciousness and persecution brought about by lack of confidence. Reconsider your point of view and see if it is truly rational.

40. *Preferred Answer = No:* Those who feel a compulsion to trade every day are victims of the market. Their "addiction" is often a mark of poor self-control which accompanies lack of positive self-esteem and winning attitudes. Vacations are a necessary part of every business. You answered "yes" and this suggests that your approach to trading may be less than successful.

41. *Preferred Answer = Yes:* If others believe that you are a methodical person, then your chances of success are good. You are most likely equally organized, precise, structured, and methodical about your investments. These are all qualities which comprise the success syndrome.

42. *Preferred Answer = Yes:* This is another positive quality. The ability to wait for a signal indicates patience. Patience is one of the key elements of profitable investing. You score one point toward successful market psychology.

43. *Preferred Answer = No:* It is not uncommon to lose faith in your trading system, particularly after several losses. In fact, you seem to be suffering from the same basic weakness that over 90% of all traders exhibit. Your "yes" answer suggests that this problem may be seriously limiting your performance.

44. *Preferred Answer = No:* If you allow your market studies to fall behind more than once or twice per year, then you are not following the road to successful investing. Typically, you will lose interest due to losses or poor decisions. This is not a healthy course of action and is often one of the first danger signs.

45. *Preferred Answer = Yes:* Your outlook is positive. You have confidence and expectations that you will succeed. This characterizes many successful investors. Keep up that winning attitude.

46. *Preferred Answer = Yes:* This is a common experience. Many investors and traders find that any change in their first decision is not a wise one. You realize this. Such awareness is often associated with market success.

47. *Preferred Answer = No:*   Unless you are one of the very few exceptional traders who can be successful acting on "gut feelings," your approach is not a good one. Most likely, you have experienced more losses than profits by acting in this way. A change should be considered. If, however, this method has been working for you, do not abandon it since it may reflect your unusual sensitivity to market events. Be suspicious, however, and watch yourself every time such decisions are made.

48. *Preferred Answer = Yes:*   You are correct. Virtually any trading system can make its user money if it is accompanied by a sound program of self-discipline and money management.

49. *Preferred Answer = No:*   Quite clearly this is a serious drawback to your performance. The reasons may be many and varied. Among them are: lack of confidence; lack of positive attitude; anxiety; poor self-discipline; unwillingness to succeed; and/or personal difficulties (home life, etc.).

50. *Preferred Answer = No:*   You might want to consider either a prolonged vacation from the market, or an evaluation of your emotional involvement by a professional. Clearly you have an unhealthy relationship with and response to the market. Since it also extends to your working life there is even more reason to consider a drastic change in behavior as a means to improvement.

15

Coping
with Stress

Progress and prosperity bring with them many wonderful things. But the things that money and success can buy, as well as the process by which they are acquired, are natural producers of great stress. In our modern society we have been increasingly inflicted with the very obvious consequences of stress which penetrate the most basic structures in our home, in our work, and even our leisure. Stress, in its various forms, has been found to be one of the most insidious and subversive killers known to humankind. The consequences of stress are not only physical and emotional, but physiological, biochemical, and financial.

So important has the topic of stress become in the free world societies, that literally thousands of books, stress management courses, and hundreds of medical procedures have been devised to detect, change, and manage its manifestations. The most obvious physical and psychological expressions of stress include high blood pressure, a host of gastric misfunctions, heart attacks, poor diet, alcoholism, drug abuse, and a host of psychiatric symptoms. More recently, stress has been related to various types of cancer and even psychopathic behavior.

One of the most significant stimuli in the syndrome of stress development is one's financial situation. Whether the stress arises from the lack of financial means or the abundance of financial ability, the ultimate product is usually the same. Whether in striving to make ends meet, or in striving to acquire more and more wealth, the individual places himself or herself in a situation certain to create many ultimately serious consequences. We have probably all heard about "type A" behavior and its consequences. We are all familiar with the expressions used as warnings to those who work under great stress for extended periods of time. "Slow down," "take it easy," "don't kill yourself," "you can't take it with you," and "get away from it all," are just a few of the things we tell ourselves and others when we recognize that stress is beginning to take its toll. And yet, although we are all fairly good at recognizing stress in others, we tend not to recognize it in ourselves. Why is this so? Why is it that we are often so good at recognizing things in others that we either refuse to accept or refuse to recognize in ourselves? How can we change this?

I believe that in addition to the physical and emotional consequences of stress, there can also be investment consequences. The individual who is in a constant state of stress, may perform better than the individual who is less tense. However, in the long run, the consequences of continued stress and pressure may be sufficiently negative, physically and emotionally, to make all positive consequences of investing virtually useless. The management of stress, therefore, is just as important in the investment world as it is in the business world at large and in one's personal life. In order to change the potential negative consequences of this very serious reality, it is necessary first to recognize that stress is taking its toll. After stress has been recognized and realized to be undesirable, steps can be taken to either minimize its consequences, or totally eliminate its serious side effects. The suggestions I'm about to offer may not necessarily be applicable for all investments and traders, but I suspect that even if they are not directly applicable to your situation, they may provide you with direction and insight about what you can do to improve your own situation. There are many courses, seminars, and training classes conducted throughout the country (and throughout the world) who teach specific techniques of stress management and stress control. I will discuss some of these in the present chapter.

First, however, let's see if we can identify and recognize situations which are apt to produce stress for the investor and how such situations can be handled.

WHAT CAUSES INVESTORS STRESS?

There are three aspects to investment stress. The first is stress that comes as a result of losses. The second is the stress that comes from profits. The third is stress that comes from or originates from a source external to the marketplace. In the first situation, stress that comes from riding losses is fairly typical among all sorts of investors. Although not easily dismissed, such stress can be managed. The second aspect of stress is that of how one deals with profits. Many individuals become quite nervous when they are either riding large profits, or when they have had a number of profits in succession. The third type of stress does not originate with the markets. It originates from one's interpersonal life with family, friends, or business. Although this stress did not originate or emanate from investment related problems, it may be further aggravated by what is taking place in one's investment life. Furthermore, if one's investment life produces only minimal stress, its effects may be cumulative, thereby, making this individual more likely to show a variety of responses to relatively small levels of stress in other areas of life.

At this point it is very important to differentiate between stress and reasonable levels of pressure which occur as a natural function of life. I believe that, even for the most well-adjusted individual, it is virtually impossible to totally eliminate the effects of stress in our modern society. If this is what you are attempting to achieve, then you will probably be better off dropping out of society and moving to the back woods. Perhaps you could join a commune whose ideals are socialistic and nonaggressive. This will probably go a long way to virtually eliminate most stress from your life. This, however, is inconsistent with investing. Stress, like many of the other behaviors and emotions discussed in this book, only becomes serious if it reaches a high level and is not properly vented. Were the effects of stress limited only to possible physical and emotional consequences, things would be bad enough. However, this is not the case. Stress can have a significantly negative effect on profits. Though it is true that small levels of anxiety and/or stress can actually improve performance and "the survival instinct," it is also true that considerably high levels of stress can decrease performance by increasing errors. Anxiety, fear, tension, extreme pressure, and their associated psychophysiological correlates are, therefore, the enemies of successful speculation and the investor/trader must do everything possible to keep stress in check. The old excuse "I do my best work under pressure" may in fact be true, however, only to a limited extent. What I am saying is that stress is only productive up to a reasonable limit. Beyond the limit, health, performance, and judgment can suffer markedly.

HOW CAN STRESS BE RECOGNIZED?

In order to deal with stress, it is important to recognize it. How can this be done? There are many people who, fortunately, cannot tolerate much stress before they begin to get physical indications that all is not right. The most common bodily symptoms are gastric and digestive disorders such as ulcers, colitis, headaches, heart palpitations, general tiredness or malaise, difficulty in sleeping, frightening dreams, and so on. Among the less observable, more insidious symptoms are such things as high blood pressure, hormonal changes, increase in errors, defective judgment, less ability to tolerate small setbacks and failures, increase in psychological symptoms such as temper, aggression, depression, and frustration.

WHAT TO DO ABOUT STRESS

The methods for coping with stress are many and varied. Coping with stress is very much an individual matter; however, I can provide you with some general guidelines based upon my own experiences and the conclusions of available stress research. The following are some suggestions:

1. Stop excessive stress before it starts. This can easily be done by taking some of the time-tested advice such as vacation regularly, work no more than a certain reasonable number of hours per day or days per week.

2. Don't try to trade every market. Attempt to specialize in certain markets. Try to become an expert in a few things. The pressure of attempting to follow all markets at all times eventually proves very stressful even to the most intelligent and capable of human beings.

3. Don't try to catch every move. The reasoning is similar to Item 2. Markets have many moves on a daily, weekly, and intraday basis. It is not possible to catch every one. Specialize in one or two, perhaps three different time perspectives and attempt to do each of these well. However, don't try to catch every move . . . it will frustrate you and add to your stress.

4. Don't set your goals too high. Achievement is a wonderful thing indeed! Having great expectations and ambitious goals are consistent with positive mental health. However, make your goals realistic. Don't attain your goal only to kill yourself in the process. It is, therefore, very important to set goals which are realistic within terms of your ability.

5. Don't take the market home with you. Trading is a very stressful occupation, particularly if you're a broker or full time trader. When the day is done, leave the market at the office. Many people like to talk and think about the market while they're away from it. I think you will significantly reduce your potential for stress if you forget about the market when the work day is over, beginning each day with a fresh look.

6. Find a way to vent stress and pressure. Perhaps the best way to cope with stress is to reduce it by venting it. One of the best ways to do this is through a regular program of

physical exercise. Whether this means sports, jogging, or aerobics, it is important to give stress a method of escape. Not only will you be doing your circulatory system great good, but you will take off pounds and relieve stress all at the same time.

7. If you cannot deal with stress, seek professional advice. You might consult a psychologist, psychiatrist, or biofeedback expert.

16

The Psychology of Prices

Jesse Livermore, writing under the pen name of Edwin Lefevre, observed that price levels appear to have important psychological significance to investors and speculators. Many investors perceive the crossing above or the falling below of certain price levels to be a significant indication of strength or weakness in the marketplace. Frequently, when such levels are penetrated, there is a flurry of activity in the given stock or commodity. In addition, a new high and new low for a given period of time often appears to be psychologically significant, frequently resulting in a great deal of emotional buying or selling. In his book, *Reminiscences of a Stock Operator*, Livermore observed the following: "It was an old trading theory of mine that when a stock *crosses 100 or 200 or 300 for the first time the price does not stop at the even figure but goes a good deal higher, so that if you buy it as soon as it crosses the line it is almost certain to show you a profit.*"* Livermore's experiences are probably just as true in today's markets as they were in years past. I have found that the psychology of prices is just as important as the psychology of the trader. After all, what is it that makes prices?

*Lefevre, Edwin. *Reminiscences of a Stock Operator*. (Larchmont, N. Y.: American Research Council, 1965, p. 101.)

Traders make prices and by making prices, traders react to prices in a seemingly never ending circle of stimulus and response. I'm reminded of the Greek Myth about Oroborous, the snake who chased his tail and finally caught it thereby consuming himself. In a similar way, traders chase prices and prices chase traders.

There is often a most interesting and observable psychological response, not only to the penetration of certain price levels in commodities and stocks, but also in the penetration of long-standing highs and lows. Figures 16.1, 16.2, and 16.3 clearly illustrate a number of such situations, lending further credence to the supposition made by Lefevre many years ago. Figures 16.4 through 16.6 show several instances of price penetration of long-standing highs.

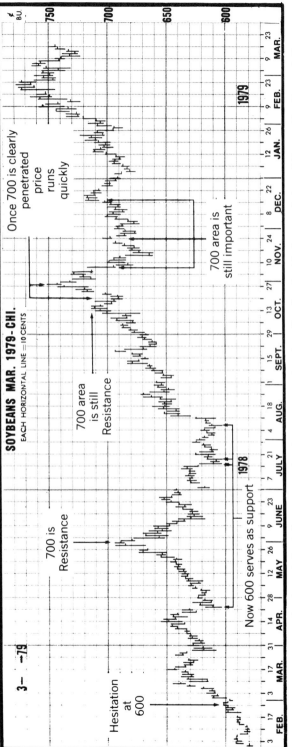

Figure 16.1. An example of psychological support and resistance at certain prices (Reprinted with the permission of Commodity Research Bureau, 79 Montgomery Street, Jersey City, N.J.)

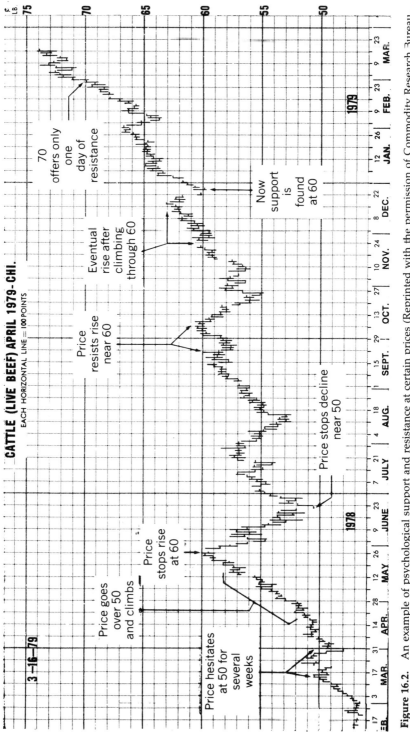

Figure 16.2. An example of psychological support and resistance at certain prices (Reprinted with the permission of Commodity Research Bureau, 79 Montgomery Street, Jersey City, N.J.)

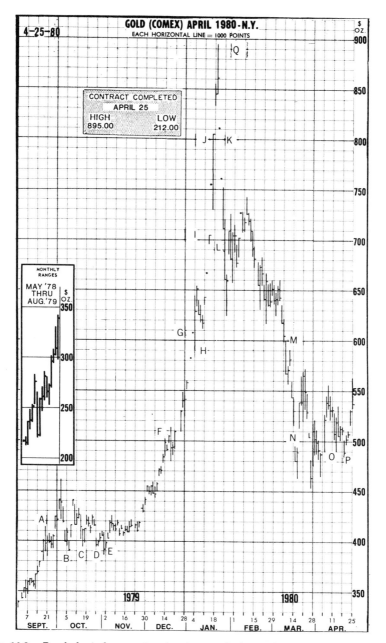

Figure 16.3. Psychological support and resistance during major price move in gold futures (Explanatory notes are on page 159) (Reprinted with the permission of Commodity Research Bureau, 79 Montgomery Street, Jersey City, N.J.)

157

Figure 16.4. How Prices Behave at Important Long Term Psychological Price Levels—London Cash Gold 1969–1978 (Explanatory notes are on page 159) (Reprinted with the permission of Commodity Research Bureau, 79 Montgomery Street, Jersey City, N.J.)

Explanatory notes for Figure 16.3

At point A prices ran into resistance at 400. Thereafter they penetrated and rallied quickly. On the subsequent decline, the 400 area served as support (points B, C, D, and E). Once 400 was clearly penetrated again, a rapid rise to 500 was seen. At 500 there was some resistance for about four–five days. When 500 was clearly penetrated, a rapid rise to 600 was seen (G). On a brief setback (H), prices then found support at 600. They then rallied quickly to 700 (I). They showed no resistance either at 700 or at 800 (J). Therefore, when prices topped at Q they fell rapidly through 800 (K) and then found only minimal support at 700 (L). Minimal support was also seen at 600 (M) on the decline since it did not provide much resistance on the rally (G). When prices declined to 500 (N), an area where they had previously found good resistance (F), they based, finding support (O and P). As a point of information, the all time high to the time of this writing was 895 in the April 1980 COMEX GOLD futures contract . . . . that's just 5 short of 900, another round number.

Explanatory notes for Figure 16.4

At $40 price showed some resistance (A). Once it passed through the $40 area a quick rise to $60 was seen. At (B), prices showed some hesitation and fell back to support at the round number of $60 (C). They then rallied to $80, passed through it for several weeks (D) and then fell back to support at the round number $80 (E). Prices ran quickly through $100, a very important psychological resistance area. The price rise through $100 was quick and the decline back to psychological support in the $100 area was also quick (G). As a point of interest, once back through the congestion high at (G), prices ran almost uninterrupted on top at (H), within a few dollars of $200/oz., another round number area. The subsequent correction brought prices down to within several dollars of $100/oz. at (I). Though psychological support and resistance at round number levels and at historical highs or lows seems to have validity it is *not*, of course, accurate or meaningful in every instance.

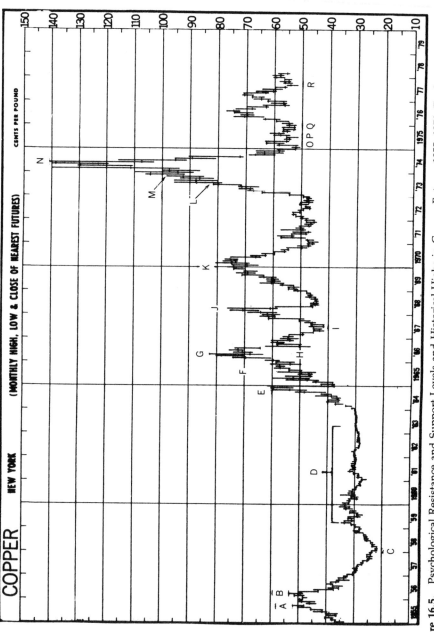

Figure 16.5. Psychological Resistance and Support Levels and Historical Highs in Copper Futures 1955–1978 (Explanatory notes are on page 162) (Reprinted with the permission of Commodity Research Bureau, 79 Montgomery Street, Jersey City, N.J.)

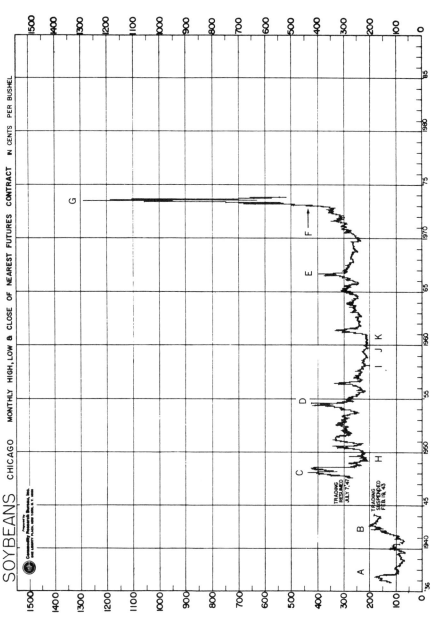

Figure 16.6. Psychological Support and Resistance Levels and Historical Highs in Soybean Futures 1936–1970 (Explanatory notes are on page 162) (Reprinted with the permission of Commodity Research Bureau, 79 Montgomery Street, Jersey City, N.J.)

161

Explanatory notes for Figure 16.5

At levels (A) and (B) prices found resistance in the 50 area (i.e., 50¢/lb.). They fell to (C), just about round 20, a round number area. They rallied and found resistance for a number of years in the 40 area (D), but once clearly through it they ran relatively quickly to resistance at (E) in the round number 60 area. They found only minor resistance at 70 (F) and topped just above 80 (G). They then fell to round number support areas (H, I). Tops were then made again in the round number area of 80 (J, K). Several years later prices penetrated tops (G, J, and K) at point (L) and then ran quickly to (M) at 100 where some resistance was seen. Once the 100 level was penetrated a move to 140 (N) followed. After topping, a large drop was seen and prices then found support a number of times in the 51–53 area, just above 50 (O, P, Q, and R).

Explanatory notes for Figure 16.6

At points (A) and (B) 200 (i.e., 200¢/bushel or $2/bushel), prices found resistance several times. After trading resumed they ran quickly to the round number area of 400–450, fell and found support in the 200 area (H). They then rose to resistance area of 400 (D) and fell again to round number support area of 200 (I, J, and K). They rallied again to resistance of 400 (E), and at (F) when they clearly penetrated previous 400–450 area resistance prices ran to a high of just under 1300 (G), another round number area!

As you can see, a trader's immediate response to penetration of historic highs or of highs that have been unpenetrated for a significant period of time (i.e., several years) can be quite dramatic. How can the investor use this psychology to his or her advantage, as opposed to being taken advantage of by the mass hysteria frequently accompanying such price penetration? First, you will observe from my examples (See notations on Figures 16.1 through 16.6) that penetration of important support or resistance level is frequently followed by a price reaction back to the original breakout point. The wise investor will not follow the first penetration, but rather will await a secondary reaction upon which to take the desired position. Very aggressive traders often take positions contrary to the penetration. A second way to take advantage of such situations is to carefully select price entry levels (if your technique employs orders at specific prices for entry and exit). In other words, if you are long in a particular market from the 280 area, for example, you might be wise to place your sell orders slightly below 300 or a fairly good amount above 300 since the market will probably encounter resistance before it gets to that level. If the market shoots through that level, it will probably move considerably higher rather quickly. A third way to take advantage of such psychology in the marketplace is to put buy or sell stop orders above the important psychological price, or below it, anticipating a very quick mover, with the objective of being out of the position very soon after your buy or sell stop has been filled. This will allow you to take advantage of quick moves on psychological penetrations.

OTHER EXAMPLES OF HOW THE PSYCHOLOGY OF PRICES OPERATES

Individuals also have a psychological response to prices that they consider to be either too high or too low. The Westerner, in particular, is more concerned about getting a bargain than he or she is about following the trend. All too often, we tend to ignore markets in strong trends because we feel the price is much too high or low and that we might be taking too much risk in buying (very little risk in buying when prices are extremely cheap). It has been said that prices are never too low to begin selling or too high to begin buying. Although I would not necessarily agree with this statement in its entirety, I think that many of us would be better off if we remembered it when we chose to ignore signals from our system. Trading systems, charts, and computers don't know anything about "cheap or expensive." Unless we are working with indicators of "overbought" or "oversold," these terms really have no importance in the trading systems. Trading systems only know buying and selling. I think it is very important that one's judgment on prices of being "too cheap" or "too expensive" not enter into your trading decisions. The final trading decision should be made on the basis of your system.

Why is it that people strive for bargains and avoid what they consider to be costly? On the basis of behavioral learning theory, it seems to me that these are learned behaviors. In Western society's search for the bargain, quality is often ignored. Although it is wise to be frugal, the market does not necessarily reward frugality. The stock and futures markets are not "supermarkets." Bargains *can* be had in the financial markets; however, it takes the eye and training of a shrewd player to know when things are under or over valued. Because the markets are so big, bargains or good sales rarely last a long time. There are literally millions waiting to jump in when a bargain appears. Professionals such as floor traders, specialists, money managers, and independent investors are always waiting on the sidelines for these rare and fleeting opportunities. Therefore, to believe that you are getting a bargain when you buy at a very cheap price; that you are making a good sale when you sell at a very high price; that you are doing a wise thing when you avoid buying at a high price; or that you are doing a very wise thing when you buy at a very low price, is not necessarily the kind of thinking that will produce consistent profits.

BOTTOM PICKING—TRYING TO BUY TOO CHEAP/TOP PICKING—TRYING TO SELL TOO HIGH

Along with the very common practice of attempting to buy into a market at too low a price or attempting to sell out of a market at too high a price, are the ever popular behaviors called top and bottom picking. The psychology of top and bottom picking is more in tune with the psychology of gambling than it is with the technique of good investing. While it is true that prices eventually reach a level which is either too high or too low, price alone cannot be the sole determinant of when this has occurred.

If your trading system happens to select purchase of a commodity or a security that is low in price, then be pleased and look forward to a potentially good percentage return. On the other hand, if your trading system has signaled the sale of something high-priced, don't be dissuaded simply because the market is so strong. In either case, it does no good to take refuge in the belief that just because the price is right, then the investment or speculation must be right. I have found that price in and of itself cannot be the only guideline upon which decisions on the marketplace are made. We need indicators to verify change in price trends, whether these indicators be technical, fundamental, a combination of the two, or otherwise, price itself can be misleading. Once again, we go back to the old rules that have been discussed so many times throughout this book. If you stick to the rules, if you make your calculations and plans ahead of time, and if you know your direction before you start, you will fare well. As I have stated frequently in this book, planning your trades and trading your plans will help you avoid a majority of errors in the marketplace.

Top picking has probably not been defined in any market text of which I am aware. Therefore, a definition is in order. By top picking, I mean the behavior of attempting to sell short in a market that is high priced simply as a function of its high price and the belief, feeling, or expectation that prices must fall because of their high level. Frequently, there is very little technical or fundamental evidence to warrant such a position. Remember that I am distinguishing between short selling at a high price where indicated by one's system, and "top picking." Generally top picking can be identified by only minimal technical evidence of a top. Commonly, top picking will occur when bullish consensus data becomes very high and many individuals expect a top. Expectations, however, are not necessarily consistent with signals from a trading system or, for that matter, with any market reality. It is very difficult to know that a top has been made or is being made until after that top has been made. Only the rare individual has the expertise, knowledge, and psychological strength to sell short at a major top without being forced out of his position by fear of an incorrect decision.

17

Some Practical
Guidelines

There is nothing I have experienced in my lifetime that can be as humbling or elating as the markets. The market can make you feel powerful, excited, ambitious, motivated, and wealthy. The market can make you feel small, depressed, rejected, picked on, deflated, and even physically ill. As you can see, the market has tremendous potential, both good and bad; however, I would be leading you astray if I told you that the market can somehow do all of these things to you without you being a direct participant in the process. Therefore, when you say such things as "How has the market been treating you?" or, "The market's really been bad, hasn't it?" or, for that matter, any other number of expressions commonly used to rationalize poor performance, be aware of the fact that the market can only do to you what you allow it to do, and even then the market can't be blamed since you alone are responsible for what occurs. The sooner you accept full responsibility for what happens to you in the marketplace, the sooner you will develop a mature attitude towards your trading and investing. By taking responsibility, you will benefit directly from your victories as well as from your defeats. The process of change must begin somewhere. We must be willing to take that initial step to change bad behaviors. We must be willing to take that first decisive action to begin the battle against losses and trading errors. But we are not alone. Although we may strive to isolate ourselves from others in making our trades and decisions, we still need the help and cooperation of others if we are to be successful at changing losing ways into winning strategies. The best way for me to end this book is to provide you with some common sense, logical, practical, and workable solutions to difficulties which you may now be encountering in the markets and/or to difficulties which you may encounter when you begin the process of change. Most of what I am about to tell you comes from long and hard practical experience and through my observation of traders and investors since the early 1970s.

SOME THOUGHTS ON PAYING ATTENTION TO THE NEWS

It's been said that "If you can keep your head while all those around you are losing theirs, you probably haven't heard the news." This is a most interesting way of saying that you are probably better off not hearing the news since the news can often cause you to commit an error in the market. I believe that only the strongest traders and investors can pay attention to the news, and that most individuals who are heavily involved in the market should probably do everything they can to isolate themselves from current events. This poses an interesting problem to the investor or trader, because society looks askance at such behavior. In particular, those who are not informed about the market frequently believe that in order to be successful you *must* know what the news is at any point or time. Whether this news happens to be company earnings, world events, government reports, and so on, the general public believes that somehow being informed of such items is consistent with or highly correlated with success. This is probably not true. The only real news that can lead to successful investing is inside news, and "inside" news is not really news. The chances are that no matter what the news happens to be you won't benefit by responding to it and you may, in fact, benefit by responding contrary to it. I can recall very few instances in my lifetime when knowing the news and paying attention to it was any value in my trading. I would venture to say that many other investors and traders have observed the same phenomenon. I believe it takes a very strong person to admit to the fact that the news is almost totally useless when it comes to investing, and in fact, knowledge of the news may be counterproductive. This is the basis on which contrary opinion works, and I think you would do well to seriously consider whether you want to pay attention to the news while you are trading the market, particularly, if most of your trading is done on an intraday basis. Knowing the news can actually have a bad psychological effect on the trader or investor because those of us who are not strong enough to ignore information contrary to what we may be doing in the marketplace, may be seriously affected by such information. As a general rule I would advise most technical traders to pay as little attention to the news as possible. For the purpose of determining what the majority thinks and then, perhaps, doing the opposite, knowledge of the news is necessary. However, the main consideration is that the news can have an unconscious effect on our decision-making process.

SOME THOUGHTS ON CONTRARY OPINION

I've already spoken about the use of contrary opinion and bullish consensus in trading and investing. Many people have attempted to systematize contrary opinion. The efforts of R. Earl Hadaday are particularly noteworthy in this area. Many of us can only use contrary opinion information as a confirming indicator and not as the sole determinant of our decision making. Contrary opinion is nothing more, nothing less, than a market indicator. At any point in time, it provides an assessment of market sentiment based on a specific method or method of survey. Although the figures on contrary opinion are valuable indeed, often there is too much anticipation in regard to the figures and their interpretations. Regardless of the measure which is being observed, I have found that there is not a 100% correlation between extremely high or low levels of bullish consensus and market movement. I have found that sometimes contrary opinion works in an almost contrary way. What I mean is that if a majority of investors or traders expect that a market will top or bottom due to extremely high or low level of bullish consensus, then the top or bottom may become a self-fulfilling prophecy and by virtue of their expectations the top or bottom will develop because of premature buying or selling. Let me see if I can illustrate for you precisely how this works. In other words, there are exceptions to the contrary opinion rule, and although contrary opinion essentially measures attitudes and provides an index of psychological forces in the markets, contrary opinion data must be used carefully. The main point is that attitudes and opinions do not always reflect behavior at a given point in time. Intentions and opinions which are expressed in a survey or in a newsletter do not necessarily represent actions that have been taken. Therefore, if the overwhelming opinion is that gold prices are going lower, this does not necessarily indicate that a bottom is imminent. It merely indicates that many people are bearish. It is not until the majority has sold out their positions or gone short in the market that we are likely to bottom. Therefore, if you are following bullish consensus, contrary opinion, or any of the other measures that evaluate the psychological state of those who trade the market, you must remember to use a combination of contrary opinion and timing. Watch for indications that will confirm a turn in the market.

WHAT TO DO ABOUT PRESSURE

There are many ways to deal with pressure in the marketplace. Some of these have been covered in Chapter 7. Here are a few helpful hints that may be of value in coping with the pressures and stresses of investing. It should be understood that these pressures are considerably greater for short-term traders than for those who are investors or those who trade for the longer term.

WAYS TO DEAL WITH PRESSURE

1. *Step Away from the Markets for a While.* This is particularly true if your short-term trading has not been producing the desired results. Sometimes leaving the markets will relieve the pressure and provide you with a new perspective when you return. How long you leave is your choice. However, I would recommend you not return to trading until you feel refreshed or energized. Many people do not realize that trading the markets is a very demanding task. We need the time to get away from the pressure, particularly when we feel that the pressure may be causing some bad decisions.

2. *Take Vacations.* I am one of the guilty individuals who does not take too many vacations. Only in recent years have I begun to realize that this is not a good thing. I have learned that even a small vacation can be very helpful—a day or two away from the pressure of trading or investing. This is very important. Many times you come back with a new perspective on the markets as well as more energy.

    I think it is important to take vacations when you are ahead in the market or when things are going well. This way you can fully enjoy your free time. If you decide to take a vacation when things are going poorly you may not be able to enjoy yourself. Reserve brief breaks from the market for periods when the pressure gets too great. Reserve vacations for times when things are going well.

3. *Take Breaks.* I find that if you are staying in close touch with the market on a tick by tick basis, it is generally a good idea to take breaks during the day. Go for a walk. Get some fresh air. Don't sit in front of the machine watching prices every minute of the day. Your energy level will quickly drop, because paying close attention to the market consumes a great deal of energy.

4. *Watch What You Eat.* There is a great tendency for individuals under pressure to "eat on the run" and to have poor eating habits. I think there are many foods you can eat that

will not burden your body and reduce your energy, but will be compatible with your digestive system, allowing you to have more energy. I am not a dietician, but I know from personal experience that this is true.

5. *Exercise.* Tension can frequently be relieved by exercise. After a very difficult day at the market go to your health or recreation club. Treat yourself to a steam bath, a sauna, a whirlpool bath, or even a massage. This helps relieve much of the muscle tension which can afflict very active traders. There are many other ways to relieve tensions. Techniques such as bio-feedback, transcendental meditation, systematic relaxation, and so forth are all good methods. Each individual should strive to develop and maintain his or her own method of coping with stress. This pertains to stress generated by the everyday pressures of trading, as well as to social and family life. Relieve your pressure before it affects your trading.

HOW TO DEAL WITH FEAR AND GREED

Fear and greed are two emotions which are universal among traders. Whether you are an investor, a speculator, or a businessperson not involved in the markets as yet, you know without a doubt what can happen when you become too greedy or too fearful. The old motto, "bulls and bears make money, but pigs don't" is very cute, but not helpful. To simply tell you that fear and greed are potentially destructive responses in the markets will not stop you from being fearful or greedy. The best way to avoid these emotions is by staying with your system. Be consistent and you will avoid emotional decisions.

SOME THOUGHTS ON BEING INDEPENDENT

I have previously made the point that independence in the marketplace is not only a virtue, but frequently, a necessity. There is a great temptation to overcome insecurity and anxiety by huddling together with others who have the same opinions as us. This group instinct is not necessarily helpful in the market. It can lead us to hold onto positions which show losses. Perhaps, the best way to overcome our need for dependency is by fighting feelings of insecurity with market facts. Whenever you become insecure, take a look at the performance of your trading system. Take care and observe how well your trading system can work. If you stick to the rules, you will easily overcome your need to give serious consideration to the assistance and opinions of others.

It often is helpful to keep a notebook or diary of daily events concerning your trading or investing. I recall instances where my need to seek shelter and comfort caused me to align myself with those sharing similar opinions. The end result was a loss. I can also recall situations where I fought the temptation to become dependent. I was handsomely rewarded for sticking to my guns. We all know that investing and speculating are endeavors which involve risk as well as the probability of being incorrect. We must remember that to give into feelings of insecurity and uncertainty will cause us to learn behaviors which are not compatible with consistently profitable performance.

THE BEST DEFENSE IS A STRONG OFFENSE

Success in the market often spoils the successful. I've frequently observed the "rags to riches, and riches to rags" stories so common in the market. Why is it that some individuals achieve quick and considerable success, only to fail miserably, losing everything they have achieved, and perhaps, more, shortly thereafter? In many instances, sudden success and failure are viewed with scorn and ridicule by those who feel that the stock and futures markets are merely a gambler's haven. They use stories such as these to support their contention that it is not possible to make and keep money in the markets. They reason that if an individual can make and lose so quickly, then there must be nothing sensible or rational about the market.

How do things like this happen? Is it true that speculation in the marketplace is nothing more than a game of chance? Is it also true that the markets are nothing more than a gambler's den? Why is it that the same individuals who have made fortunes can frequently lose their fortunes? I believe the answer to these questions is threefold. First, individuals who achieve "instant" success do so through either chance, or a combination of chance and strict adherence to good trading principles. Second, as the profits mount, there is a great tendency to forget the trading rules which assisted the rise to profits, or for the good luck to run out and the profits to deteriorate. Third, as profits increase, there is a tendency to increase risk taking and gambling with the profits. The process is a simple one indeed. As human beings, we are all vulnerable to the self-destruction which can result from such behaviors.

The individual who achieves success through good fortune but who is not aware of the many rules and procedures outlined in this book will sooner or later (most likely sooner) become vulnerable to the "misfortune" of not following trading rules. The tendency for failure increases as the rise to success accelerates. They are aspects at the opposite end of the same continuum. When an individual loses sight of rational trading principles, good judgment, and sound investment techniques, whether a long-term or short-term trader, he or she is opening the door to possible failure by lowering his or her defenses. The consistent winners in the markets are always on the defensive. They avoid the trading blunders that frequently occur when we are "looking the other way."

The answer to avoiding sudden "attack" in the market is to consistently remain aware of your objectives, rules, positions, strengths, weaknesses, assets, liabilities, capabilities, vulnerabilities, and a host of other factors which comprise a profitable trading and investing program. One good way to remain in touch with all of the above (and more) is to take a regular assessment of your situation and direction. Reinforce your understanding of the rules. Review your successes and failures, but in particular review the reasons why, and the methods by which you have succeeded and/or failed.

Failures are just as important as successes. Perhaps, failures are even more important than successes in the learning process. By reviewing your failures, you make yourself less vulnerable to future failure. Although we may fail for different reasons at different times, the knowledge of where we went wrong each time will help us avoid committing the same blunder in the future. You must keep your defenses high because the enemy will strike when you least expect it. The enemy, by the way, is you.

THOUGHTS ON STICKING TO A SCHEDULE

Hopefully, by now you have had a good opportunity to assess your strengths and weaknesses. You know what's responsible for your successes and what's responsible for your failures. I find that the single greatest area of deficiencies among investors and speculators is a lack of organization and schedule. It is probably true that this organizational/scheduling deficit is a reflection of personality and daily life itself. The way you are in your personal life is how you tend to be when it comes to investment and speculation. Because a schedule is so important, I offer these suggestions:

1. *Account for Most of Your Time.*   When you make your schedule account for all of your time during the day, you don't have to schedule every waking minute of the day, but make sure that most of your time is accounted for, including a description of what you do during each time period. Once you examine the list of what you have been doing each day of the week, you will find there are many ways you can either save time, plan your time more economically, or eliminate certain wasteful things you are doing.

2. *Don't Spend too Much Time on the Market.*   You may be surprised by this statement but I believe there is such a thing as spending too much time on the markets. Don't get carried away. I honestly don't believe that it takes more than four to six hours per week for the average invester to study the marketplace and his or her particular investment or speculative investment. I include in this time the preparation of charts, graphs, indicators, computations, and so on. If you are a

market professional and are in touch with the market all day as your primary occupation, then I strongly suggest you leave your work at the office.

There is plenty of time during the working day both before, during, and after market hours to do whatever is necessary to do market analysis. If you're spending too much time studying the market during the day, then I think an investment in a computer would be a good idea, since it can cut the work load considerably.

3. *Make Your Schedule Realistic.* If you set goals that are too ambitious you are setting yourself up for failure. When you make your schedule, establish simple goals you know you can achieve. It is much better to succeed at something simple than to fail at something which is totally beyond your capabilities. As you become successful with your schedule and expectations, you can add new responsibilities and expectations. At first, however, keep it simple!

4. *Evaluate Your Progress.* After several weeks or days, evaluate your progress. This is done by keeping a daily diary of your activities and comparing it to your planned schedule. Compare the two. See how closely you are sticking with your schedule. If there are discrepancies, then take the necessary action to correct them. Remember that you do not want to stray from your schedule too much. If you achieve much more than has been scheduled in a particular area of activity, then you are probably neglecting something else. You may be concentrating too much effort in one area. Try to stick with your original plans. After demonstrating to yourself that you can stick to a schedule, make the necessary changes and adjustments.

5. *Try to Get Help with Your Schedule.* Many times a difficult or unpalatable task is made more tasteful by recruiting the help of a friend. Find someone who is also interested in learning to work by a schedule. With two people participating, the avenue for analysis and feedback is opened, and the process can be a much more rewarding, enriching, and profitable one.

6. *Don't Give Your Schedule Up!* After you find that your schedule has been working well, you will be tempted to give it up. You will feel that you know your daily life well enough to drop the structure. Don't do it! Within a matter of weeks, perhaps days, you will find that your efficiency and organization have declined. You will become frustrated, and you will leave the door open to costly errors of judgment and emotion in the market. If your schedule works, stick with it. Don't give it up because you think you are too good for it.

18

The Five Greatest Blunders

Of all the things that can go wrong in the market, I suspect that a good 80% of them occur as a function of the trader and not as a function of the market or the system. Although it is very tempting for us to blame our mistakes on others, whether the scapegoats be friends, family, advisors, brokers, or floor traders, the fact remains that a majority of the time we alone are responsible for the mistakes we make in the market. Even if we know we are making mistakes because of others, we are still guilty for not doing anything to stop the mistakes. Of all the mistakes that an investor can make, I suspect that a majority are a function of trader psychology. If a system is specific and tells us to "buy here," "sell there," "use a stop loss here," "take your profits there"; then there can be very little doubt as to what the system is saying or has said at any given point in time. The fact of the matter is that a signal is a signal and a trade is a trade. There should not be any degree of interpretation as to the meaning of signals when signals are clear. There should not be even the slightest moment of hesitation if the trading system says "jump." Any unwarranted delay in executing the mandates of your trading system, whether technical or fundamental, may prove costly in the long run. Although there may be instances when you are rewarded for waiting, it is likely that, over the long run, you will be punished for waiting. Why have a system if you don't use it? Trading systems are like seat belts. Most automobiles have them and most drivers don't use them. Most traders have systems, (even if loosely construed as systems) yet very few traders actually stick to the rules.

When questioned as to why the trading system rules have not been followed explicitly, every individual will have his or her excuses. Excuses can take many forms. More often than not, however, there is someone else to blame. There are hundreds of rationalizations and we have all used them at some time or another. The simple fact of the matter is that most excuses do not hold water. I can truly say that I alone have been responsible for well over 90% of my successes and failures in the market. Many times we do not see or accept personal responsibility at the precise moment, yet as time passes we begin to realize the truth. This is true in our personal lives as well as in the markets.

There are five major blunders which seem to be universal among traders and investors. These errors are so costly, so serious, so totally absurd, so common, and yet, so simple to understand, that I feel it worthwhile to spend an entire chapter explaining and discussing what they are and how they may be overcome. *Not* necessarily in order of importance, these five errors are (1) failing to take a loss at the right time, (2) failing to act on signals, (3) closing out profitable positions too soon or too late, (4) acting on extraneous input (i.e., tips, news, etc.), and (5) trading with insufficient capital. I contend that these five broad areas of trading blunders, comprise from 60 to 80% (or more) of the losses taken as a result of psychological factors. I also maintain that if we can recognize the behavioral components and the stimulus/response aspects of these behaviors, we can eliminate a large portion of our losses and replace them with profits. I will deal with each area individually, citing my understandings of the reasons behind each blunder as well as the ways in which the problems may be overcome.

FAILING TO TAKE A LOSS AT THE RIGHT TIME

What causes traders to ride losses for extended periods of time, well beyond the price level at which they should have closed out their position? There are many reasons. Perhaps understanding them will help shed some light on your own behavior.

Is It a Learned Behavior?

Since I have maintained that virtually everything that we do in life is learned, I also hold this viewpoint about the markets. Virtually all of our trading behavior is a reflection of our personality. Our personality is comprised of cumulative learning experiences that have developed from the moment of birth. Let's analyze the learning aspects of "taking a loss."

To avoid closing out a losing trade in the market, one must not exert very much effort. In an immediate sense, human beings find it much easier to do nothing than to do something. The act of taking a loss requires unpleasant thoughts, unpleasant actions, and *most of all, unpleasant consequences*. The immediate consequence of taking a loss is the report back from your broker indicating the price at which you took your loss, and in a number of days, a slip of paper in the mail stating in dollars and cents precisely how much you lost. In other words, *taking a loss has negative consequences*. These consequences are immediate and painful. To avoid taking a loss also has negative consequences; however, these consequences are *delayed*. Therefore, the individual who avoids taking a loss need not experience any immediately negative effects.

Although it is true that at a later point the pain may be much more intense than it would have been initially, the fact remains the pain has been delayed. The stimulus–response model here is very simple. The stimulus is the knowledge of your losing position. The response can be either twofold. One option is to avoid taking a loss. The eventual consequences, though negative, are not actually experienced until considerable time has passed. A second option is to take the loss quickly. The pain in this case is experienced quickly and its effects are certainly not pleasant. To review, the stimulus–response connection and the consequences of taking a loss are very specific. Although it may be more painful (i.e., greater loss) to take losses later rather than sooner, the pain is delayed and the suffering need not be immediate.

Inconsistency and Riding Losses

Earlier in the book, I talked about faulty learning and the damage it can cause. Not taking losses promptly is probably caused by inconsistent learning. Inconsistent learning is another form of random reinforcement. Random reinforcement is the occurrence of positive consequences on a random basis. In other words, the individual does not know when this response will be rewarded. The reward could come at any time. It could come soon; it could come late; it could come after 10 hours on one occasion, after six days the next, and after two years the next. Learning theorists have demonstrated that random reinforcement schedules produce the strongest learning. "Strong learning" is learning that is very resistant to forgetting (technically known as "extinction").

An example will illustrate precisely what I mean. You take a position in stock XYZ. You buy at 50. Your system says that a closing price below 46 will indicate a change in trend to the downside, and you must, therefore, close out your position. Shortly after you purchase the stock it begins to decline and drops below 46. 46 was your loss point. However, you do not exit because you "believe, feel, expect, or anticipate" that the stock will recover. The stock continues to decline. Within a matter of days it is 40, then 37. Now you rationalize that the stock is "too low" to sell out. You continue to hold. After several weeks the stock stabilizes and begins to trade between 32 and 39. This continues for several months. Your technical indicators continue bearish. Soon your indicators begin to change, and there is a signal to buy. Within a matter of days, the stock begins to move higher. Soon it is back up to 47. You continue to hold. Stock moves to 55 and to 60 and your system says to sell. This time you listen. You get out. After several months waiting, and due to a broken rule, you end up with a profit! Can you imagine that! Being rewarded for breaking the rules? You are relieved, you feel good, you know you "did the right thing." You have a profit to show for it. Isn't that wonderful? Dead wrong! Let's take a look at what really happened. It doesn't take much analysis to see that you have been rewarded for breaking the rules of your system. You haven't broken all the rules; however, you *did break an important rule.* The rule that told you to get out of your initial position was broken. Although prices eventually went your way, it is entirely possible that they may not have gone your way for quite some time. Of course, you feel good now. But what have you learned? You have learned that by holding on to a losing position and by not admitting to a loss when you should you will eventually come out with a profit. Perhaps the next time you will not be as fortunate. Perhaps there will be several next times, six or seven losing positions, all at once all of which are being held because of faulty learning that has taken place. What's worse, several of these losers may eventually go your way as well. You won't know why, how, or when to tell when they will turn around and go your way, so you learn to hold on. You hold losing positions. You further the faulty learning. What happens then? Sooner or later, most likely sooner, you will be in a position where you are holding on to a "potfull of losers." Soon all of your capital is tied up. You watch some big moves happen, but you can't participate because you have no capital. It's all tied up in losers.

You may think my scenario a bit extreme, but stop and consider it for awhile. If you do, and if you are honest with yourself, you will find, for all intents and purposes, you have probably been in a similar situation yourself. If you find yourself in such a situation now, or if you find yourself in such situations repeatedly, then you are the product of faulty learning.

Can you see how intermittent or random reinforcement shapes and perpetuates faulty learning in the market? How can you change it? The first and foremost rule about changing a losing behavior is to recognize the behavior as soon as it begins. The second rule is to change the positive consequences of the behavior immediately, so that you are not rewarded for the behavior. How do you change the positive consequences? Force yourself to stick to the rules, even if it means you must hire someone to look over your shoulder or "breathe down your neck" until you have learned self control and discipline. In addition, many of the suggestions I have made, such as having a check list, planning your day, enlisting assistance, and reviewing your progress and rules regularly, will all help.

The example of inconsistent learning I have just given is not unique to this one area of investor behavior. It applies to virtually every aspect of investor behavior and can be demonstrated as a significant cause of poor investor education.

Losses Are Ego Deflating

I contend that the behavioral explanations and learning principles given earlier are the only things necessary to fully understand why losses are not taken timely. Some people feel better, however, if these explanations are given in terms that are more "humanistic," or palatable. Psychiatrists prefer to use scientific terms and hypothetical constructs to make their explanations seem more scientific. Actually, I think that explaining things in that way complicates the matter, but since so many people seem to enjoy it, here are a few other ways of understanding the unacceptable behavior of riding losses.

Some psychologists would claim that admitting to a loss is a form of deflating one's ego. In other words, the normal individual perceives himself or herself to be strong and not subject to much error, but when a loss is incurred, it serves as a blow to one's ego ideal. On an unconscious level, the individual chooses not to act, so as to avoid admitting to feelings of fallibility.

Another way of looking at this situation is by saying that the individual has feelings of inadequacy when a trading decision results in a loss. The traditional psychoanalytical point of view would probably employ a psychosexual explanation as its standard interpretation. As you recall from our earlier discussions of psychosexual development, such Freudian terms as castration anxiety, the Oedipus complex, and the Electra complex can readily be applied to this situation. In trading the market, the individual competes against other traders. Competition is seen as a form of sexual rivalry. On a symbolic level, one could say that traders are competing for a prize, "money," which in their unconscious mind represents "power." Power, aggression, strength, sexual prowess—these all originate from the same unconscious source. Theoretically, this should be true for male or female. Therefore, if the unconscious mechanism involved in the marketplace is sexual competition, then taking a loss in the market is symbolically seen as sexual defeat. Unconsciously, some individuals may view defeat in the marketplace as symbolic castration. In their effort to avoid symbolic castration, they avoid facing the loss. I suppose that talking to these individuals, I might inquire (therapeutically, of course), "Would you rather lose all of it or some of it?" By taking your loss now, you won't lose as much as you may lose later on.

I am certain that there is at least one explanation for virtually every different personality theory. We could even seek and find religious answers, astrological answers, and a host of other explanations. What's the bottom line? To be cold, calculating, and pragmatic, the bottom line is always the same. If you don't take your losses quickly, they will probably increase. The chances of being in a losing position and having that losing position turn profitable before you are forced to get out, either through lack of funds or through emotions, are very slim indeed. Although you may escape unscathed on occasion, this is the exception rather than the rule. I maintain that it is a function of learning. Perhaps even worse than the loss that you may take is the fact that you learned a behavior that is not consistent with profitable trading.

FAILING TO ACT ON SIGNALS

One of the most serious errors a trader can commit is failure to act on signals. By signals, I mean indications to buy or sell as generated by one's trading system. Unfortunately, this blunder is not as simple as it seems. In failing to act on a signal an investor or trader leaves himself or herself open to a multitude of other possible errors. Among these are included chasing the markets, waiting for prices to retrace, panicking, and buying or selling too late. Let's see if we can list some of the reasons that this happens.

My observations lead me to the conclusion that the following reasons are instrumental in creating the backdrop for the development and perpetuation of this blunder:

1. Insecurity about the potential of one's trading system
2. Listening to too many opinions
3. Trading with limited capital, which makes for a nervous trader
4. Inability to appreciate the positive consequences of consistent and systematic trading

Most of those deficiencies are a direct function of either incomplete or faulty learning experiences. Here are some suggestions by which one can help overcome the tendency to not act on signals:

1. Enlist the help of a friend or broker who will force you to follow the rules.
2. Make a commitment to follow your rules and signals for two full weeks. The odds are that after doing this you will learn first hand the benefits of following your signals.
3. Spend some time thinking about what goes through your mind when you are faced with a decision to make a trade. Chances are that if it takes you more than one minute to react, then you are thinking too much and will probably make a mistake.

CLOSING OUT PROFITS TOO SOON OR TOO LATE

Another error committed by many traders and investors is the mistake made in holding on to a winning position too long or closing it out too soon. There are many possible explanations for this behavior. Some of these explanations are very specific to individual situations. I think, however, that three or four major explanations will account for most occurrences of these behaviors. I have frequently seen individuals with good profits end up with losses after all is said and done. For quite some time there may have been paper profits, but something happened. The individual failed to show any real profit once the position was closed out. Any good trading system will provide follow-up and stop loss techniques which will allow the individual to exit the position fairly quickly if the trend reverses. Although you may have been in this situation yourself, you still may find yourself saying, "How could anyone let a profit turn into a loss, especially a large loss?" Now, in the cold light of day, as you sit and read this book, imbued with the spirit of good sense and self knowledge, you find it difficult to believe that you would do anything so foolish, or for that matter that anyone would. Yet, I'm sure that if you think back to situations where you may have been the guilty party, you will find that a number of reasons may have been responsible for the problem. Although you may not now remember what transpired, I believe that a small anecdote might refresh your memory as to the reasoning process which is frequently hard at work in such situations.

Let's start with a hypothetical example which, although fictitious, is not outside the realm of reality. A typical investor, let's call him Joe, has been on a fairly bad losing streak. His last several trades have all produced losses. Quite naturally he feels downtrodden, dejected, depressed, lacks confidence in his system, dislikes himself, and all of the other things that usually coincide with losing money in the market. Although the feelings are all negative, the investor is persistent. Upon his very next trading signal, he assumes a long position in a given stock. Although he has very little self confidence in the position, he is pleased with himself for having followed the signal. Before too long the position begins to move in his favor. He realizes that he has a winner on his hands. He now has three choices to make. He can hold on to the position in accordance to what his system dictates; he can ignore his system and buy more of the stock, or he can sell it based on no signals. He reasons that since he has had so many losers in succession, this winner must compensate for the losers and he expects that by "doubling up" on this position, he will "milk it" for all it is worth. In this particular case the individual decides to buy more. He might have decided to "take the money and run."

If he did, then the story ends here. He has gone contrary to his system, yet he made a profit. He was rewarded for disobeying his system. Assume, however, that Joe bought more, also contrary to his system.

In some cases, Joe would not only have doubled up but tripled up, buying more stock at various points along the way. Let's see if we can understand some of the feelings and thoughts that might be going on in Joe's mind. As the stock continues to rise, Joe begins to experience an almost invincible feeling that he cannot lose because the technical action is so convincing. Frequently, this feeling will cause many an investor to ignore signals, warning signs, and indicators from his or her system. Joe begins to reason "if my system knows everything, why did it cause me to take so many losses in succession?" The feeling is, therefore, that the system is not all it should be. This type of individual will second guess the system, making his or her own rules as the purpose may fit. In this particular case, Joe could do either of two things. He could exit immediately, feeling that things have gone too far too fast. He believes that if he holds on, the system will prove to be wrong again. He could continue to hold, eventually ignoring indications from the system saying that a top may have been reached. In any event, what's transpiring here is a conscious or unconscious decision to ignore one's system. In this particular case the individual continues to hold on with unrealistic expectations that prices are headed much, much higher. I am not stating that such action will always be wrong. There are, in fact, many instances in which such a strategy (i.e., holding on to a winning position) is not a bad one at all. What has Joe done wrong? He has chosen to ignore the rules of his system, a system which he has probably put considerable time and money into, and a system which is based on his own analytical terms and, therefore, ideally does what he wants it to do. Whether it is sound strategy to hold on to winners indefinitely is not the issue here. What is at issue is the fact that Joe has broken his own rules. In doing this he not only sets precedent for further violation of the rules, but he also puts himself into a situation *whereby he will probably learn nothing whether he profits from his actions or eventually takes a loss.* Getting out too soon or getting out too late are both opposite sides of the same tarnished coin!

Let's assume the stock continues to rise, not necessarily by leaps or bounds, but in a general trend. Nothing moves straight up. The stock has its brief setbacks, but the general trend remains higher. Our investor is quite delighted since he now has definite proof that his system was wrong again—the stock that was supposed to be topping, merely reacted a few dollars lower and is now back on its upward course. Assume for the moment that the stock has more than doubled in value. Tenuously, our investor holds on expecting three hundred percent as the next milestone.

Everything seems to be going along smoothly. The trading system, however, continues to give warnings that something is wrong, and that soon the stock may top if a top has not already been seen. Then, one day, the stock which had been trading at $63 per share opens at $47, down $16. Our investor is quite upset. Understandably shaken by the sudden change of events, his first reaction is grief and great concern. He then begins to "think" about the situation. This is perhaps his biggest mistake. If he were only to take a look at his trading system, the best answer and only to his dilemma would be clear. There is only one answer, and it is the same answer that was the answer all along. That answer is to "sell out." His thinking and reasoning lead him to the conclusion that the huge price increase that occurred over the last three months was certainly not typical. The stock was vulnerable to a good "correction." "Correction" is a word that is used as an euphemism for the "market doing what we thought it would do." Our investor knows that something is definitely wrong. The stock should never have dropped that much in one fell swoop. He is concerned but he has rationalized it. What he could not rationalize he intellectualized. Now the stock is considerably lower than its highest recent price. More thought enters into the picture. Again, ignoring the trading system, Joe, who has now become trapped in a cycle of second guessing his system, decides to hold on because a brokerage firm has recommended its purchase. But in his heart, he knows he is grasping at straws. In some cases, he may decide to add to his position, thinking that if

this truly is nothing more than a correction, it would be only logical to buy more. Carrying this little story to its logical conclusion,
the stock may rally several times and each time the emotions of
fear, greed, and hope again enter into the picture. With the passage of time and the continued decline of the stock, what were
once profits have now become an emotional albatross.

Assuming that the stock continues to decline and that our
investor is loaded down with stock from higher levels, bought on
what he felt was a normal price correction, it does not take long
before the overall position shows a loss. The investor who finally
sees the light, will eventually close out the position. This will usually occur when most of the profit is gone or when there is a loss.
The investor who is unwilling to admit to what has happened will
frequently continue to hold, and, perhaps at some point may actually make a profit. Pity the poor investor who does, for he or
she has been rewarded for extremely poor performance, breaking
most of the rules, and trading by emotion.

Although I do not claim that all situations happen precisely in
this fashion, I think you will find many elements in this story
with which you can identify. Analyzing the reasons for such behavior I arrived at the following list which explains why some
investors refuse to let go of profitable positions until, in many
cases, the positions are no longer profitable.

1. Emotional rather than systematic or logical decision making
2. Insecurity about the ability of the trading system
3. Unrealistic expectations that one winning position can compensate for a series of previous losses
4. Second guessing a system
5. Interpretation of market actions based on feelings rather
   than technical or fundamental fact
6. Similar behaviors in the past which have slowly but surely
   become more serious as a function of having been rewarded

The last point is, perhaps, the most significant in terms of
understanding how such behaviors develop. You remember that

I have frequently indicated the importance of behavioral consequences. I have shown how inappropriate or unsystematic behavior in the market can actually be followed by a profit. When
something like this occurs, the person who engaged in the given
behavior is actually being rewarded for not following the system.
Although it feels good to take a profit, the reward itself has resulted in faulty learning of the type that may eventually prove to
be the undoing of the trader and his system. Learning operates
in a very subtle way. Most of the time we learn things and are not
aware that we are learning things. In the marketplace things happen so quickly that we frequently fail to stop and analyze what
has transpired. Money is a very powerful reinforcer. When we
make some money in the market, we are so overwhelmed and
overjoyed as a function of the amount we have made that we
seldom stop and question why or how this has happened. *Were
we to be more analytical in behavioral terms we would probably benefit
considerably from the knowledge that the analysis of profits and losses
would give us.* We not only want to analyze why a loss is taken but
also why a profit is taken. The best way to do this is to spend time
analyzing your successes and failures in the markets based on
notes you should take every time you trade, whether the trade is
profitable or not. You should do this until you have overcome
most of the avoidable market errors of which you have been
guilty.

ACTING ON EXTRANEOUS INFORMATION

If I had to make a judgment as to one of the most serious errors a
trader can make in the stock or commodity markets, I would say
that "acting on extraneous information" is, perhaps, the worst.
By "extraneous information" I mean *any information that is not a
direct result of signals or indicators derived from one's trading system.*
Rumors, inside information, brokers' recommendations, news,
input from other trading systems, fundamental developments,
weather, and a host of other factors are all considered extraneous
to technical analysis. For the fundamentalist, technical developments may be considered extraneous. Regardless of your system-

atic standpoint, any input that is not a direct result of your system is not systematic. It's as simple as that. Therefore, when you follow extraneous inputs, you are leaving yourself vulnerable to results which are not the creation of your trading system. You are also putting yourself into a situation which does not provide you with any knowledge or learning as a result of the losses or profits you may be taking. I have pointed out earlier that the worst learning results from profits which are made in spite of unsystematic behavior and inputs.

Let's admit to the fact that, sooner or later, 99% of us are guilty of making some trades that are not consistent with or generated by our trading system. Since we are all guilty to a greater or lesser extent, we can speak as equals and admit to our shortcomings. In so doing, we take the first step toward self-improvement. Perhaps, in understanding why we act on imputs which are extraneous to our system, we may glean some knowledge that can help remediate and, at some point in the future, totally eliminate these behaviors from our investment repertoires.

The news will often prompt you to establish a position in the market. Interestingly enough, the news will prompt the position you established to move in your favor. The immediate consequence of acting on news, tips, rumors, and so on, can frequently be a positive consequence. Therefore, we have established another situation in which the investor or trader is rewarded for not following the rules. Consider also the situation whereby a trader establishes a position based on rumor and derives a significant profit as a result of this behavior.

TRADING WITH INSUFFICIENT CAPITAL

Another blunder which is not only extremely common in the markets, but also one which has taken its toll on many traders is the error of trading with limited capital. Although it may be sad, it remains true that to make money, you need money. While some individuals have made millions starting with literally nothing, these individuals are few and far between. You would be best off not to fall into the trap of wishful thinking by looking at their examples. If there is anything to be learned from these people it is that patience, perseverance, creativity, and innovation, are probably more important start-up qualities than is a great deal of capital. However, it is best to remember that to create something, you must start with something. In the area of stock and futures trading, it is necessary to start with a sufficient amount of capital in order to increase the probability of success.

Let's examine some of the reasons that individuals have for entering the market with insufficient capital. Naturally, the most cogent reason for not trading with sufficient start-up capital, is the fact that the individual simply does not have available funds. This sounds logical; however, it does not answer a very important question. If the capital is not available, then why invest or trade? In other words, even though the new investor or trader may have been informed about the risks of using minimal capital, why did he or she behave contrary to the existing advice? The answer to this question is that such behavior derives from a combination of wishful thinking and misunderstanding. I have found that those who are new to the markets and those who do not understand what investing in the stock and commodity markets is all about, have grave misconceptions about the financial markets. Generally speaking, they feel that trading is not difficult, that making money rests on "having a good broker," that they can "take a flyer" and come out ahead, and that even though more money is necessary, they are somehow an exception to the rule.

These public misconceptions are primarily due to a lack of education. Although it may be wise and prudent to take a very small account and invest in a very small amount of stock or limited risk options, the fact remains that more capital is preferable to less capital. The simple reason for this relates to probability. It is obvious that the life expectancy of a trading or investing account will be increased if the account begins with more funds and follows a conservative and prudent money management approach. Therefore, the investor who has had all of the above explained to him and chooses to ignore it, is doing so as an expression of wish fulfillment (and other unrealistic expectations) which will lead to disappointment.

Among other excuses I have frequently heard is, "I have more money to trade with, but I want to start small, and then I will put some more money in when I have more experience." At first this sounds like good reasoning. It is certainly true that we are told not to risk more than we can afford, and we are also told to trade small and be conservative. This is all very true. I am, however, opposed to putting in only part of what you have allotted to trading.

Psychologically, these individuals will believe they are only risking what is in their accounts. This will give them too casual an attitude, and they may take chances they otherwise would not be inclined to take. If these individuals felt that their entire risk capitals were at stake, I believe that their attitudes would be significantly different. As we have seen, attitude affects behavior, and behavior affects results. What usually happens in such cases is that these individuals put in a small amount of money and take unnecessary risks, thinking that they have the security of their additional risk capital to give them confidence. Before too long, their starting amount may be gone and they dip into their additional funds. The same process may recur, and soon, perhaps half of the capital has been depleted. Now these individuals realize that a good percentage of their money is gone. They commit the balance. However, they have now become very nervous, lack self confidence, and are likely to be too conservative as they overcorrect for previous errors.

Therefore, it is important to begin with your entire starting amount, placing these funds with your broker, whether you use them or not. I am not saying that all of your risk capital should be working in the markets at all times. What I am saying is that of your available risk capital, a certain percentage should be allocated to stock and/or futures trading, and that this percentage be placed in your account in its entirety so that you will have an exact awareness of where you stand in your trading.

Another common excuse for starting with insufficient capital is that the investor has "heard of a good trade through a friend who is well connected, and this is all I have to risk." You have probably heard this type of story many times before. On the one hand this makes good sense; these individuals know exactly how much they want to risk, and since they will not take any more than this amount of risk, they are practicing very disciplined money management. On the other hand for the individual who has no experience in the markets, I don't consider such behavior "investing" or "trading" but merely "gambling." If you have the capital and temperament, then gambling may be acceptable; however, I do not believe that one should make the mistake of considering such behavior "investing" or "trading." This strategy makes the probability of investment success very low.

19

Some Further Thoughts on Long Term versus Short Term

In 1980, when I wrote *The Investor's Quotient*, the securities and futures industries were just entering a period of transition characterized by significant changes in commission structure and customer services. Over the last several years, competition among brokerage firms, particularly in the futures industry, has become quite intense and a virtual "discount war" has broken out. A number of large discount house names have emerged as the principal providers of lower rates. It is interesting to note that the trend for discount commissions occurred during a period of economic deflation and generally sideways or lower futures markets. This trend was also observed in other areas of American business. The growth of discount food retailers, the popularity of generic foods, the air fare war among airlines, and the significant decline in petroleum prices are all different aspects of the same secular trend. Is it no wonder, then, that many independent investors and speculators have either moved their accounts or opened separate accounts at discount houses?

In addition to the trend toward conservatism in the economy and society, we can clearly see that investors have become conservation minded in the area of commissions. During the same period, another most significant change swept the free world. The dramatic and virtually exponential growth of home computer systems with sophisticated capabilities and large electronic memories has revolutionized the areas of economics, finance, and business. It is now possible for the average individual to purchase and employ computer technology, which was very costly only several years ago. Furthermore, one no longer needs a degree in computer engineering or mathematics to program these marvelous machines. The programs or software that makes these machines perform their amazing feats can now be purchased in prepackaged form for thousands of applications. Prewritten software is available in virtually every area of mathematical, physical, and social sciences. Complex mathematics, statistical analysis, formula research, graphics, plotting, and accounting are all available in prewritten form for use in the home or business.

The area of stock and commodity analysis certainly has not been neglected by this rapidly growing field. In fact, there are now many publications, computer user groups, computer clubs, and data services whose speciality it is to accumulate, formulate, and disseminate data and programs for stock and commodity analysis.

The combination of computer analysis and discount brokerage has virtually revolutionized the stock and commodity industries, making previously difficult and/or costly technical and fundamental analysis within reach of the average investor. My first computer system was purchased in the late 1970s for approximately $40,000. The programming and software which were necessary to make the machine run added, perhaps, another $25,000 to the bill over several years after the computer was purchased. The service contract for repair has added approximately $4000 a year to the bill, and the purchase of data for commodity analysis has been approximately $3000 more. You can see that this was indeed a costly package. In 1985, the purchase of a computer system with many of the same capabilities, storage, and an even larger memory would cost at the maximum $10,000, perhaps

$15,000 complete. This would include much software, data, and graphics or plotting capabilities. An added feature of contemporary computer systems is their small size. My first computer system was housed in a computer room approximately 7 X 6 feet, with the machine itself being more than five feet tall. A similar system today might be no larger than several feet high by 3–5 feet deep with 2–3 feet across for the mainframe unit, and with video monitors and a machine of perhaps smaller size for printing or plotting.

A third area of dramatic growth has been the field of quotation systems. For many years, price quotes were available only to brokerage offices or to those who had mechanical ticker machines at their disposal. Now, any individual with $400–$500 a month as a fee can obtain instant quotes right in the office or home on a video screen monitor. In the last several years, new services have become available which provide the quotes, the computers, the programs, and the graphic capabilities to perform virtually all of the technical analyses that an investor or futures trader might need. By now, you may be asking yourself why I am telling you all of this. That is a very valid question. Before you conjecture any longer, I will get to the point.

Due to reasons just cited, namely, lower commissions, the affordability of computer systems, and affordability of price quotations, many things which were previously not possible or practical for the average investor have now become attainable. By lowering commissions, by improving technology, and by making both of these available to the average individual, the advantage of trading on the floor of the exchange has been diminished. It is now possible for the average individual with motivation, time, and finances to trade effectively for the short term on a daily basis. I have been a proponent of long-term trading for many years. In my books, my consultations with investors and traders, my newsletters, and my public lectures, I have repeatedly stated that short-term trading is a difficult thing to do, and it is, furthermore, not intended for or accessible to most individuals. I have matured considerably in my viewpoint. I have seen that with new technology, many things previously impossible or impractical are now possible. One of these is short-term trading.

While I still believe that short-term trading and futures trading are not for most investors, some of the reasons for avoiding short-term trading in the past are no longer applicable. Nevertheless, some of the reasons previously applicable are still valid today. I think that the best way to give you a synopsis of the current status of short-term trading in terms that relate to investor psychology is to provide you with a list of advantages as well as a list of disadvantages to short-term trading. You can then decide what is right for you. However, do not make this decision until you have studied both lists and until you have examined my third listing, which contains my evaluation of prerequisites for short-term trading.

By examining Figure 19.1, Disadvantages of Short-Term Trading, you can readily see that short-term trading is no less demanding than it ever was, in terms of time commitment. However, in terms of other factors, short-term trading is more feasible than it ever was. Some of the advantages to short-term trading, in particular so-called day trading, are shown in Figure 19.2. Figure 19.3 shows prerequisites for short-term or long-term trading.

---

1. Short-term trading seems to increase the likelihood of emotional response by placing the individual under more stress and pressure.
2. Short-term trading requires more of the time commitment than does long-term trading.
3. Short-term trading requires more attention to small price movements and thereby can result in insufficient attention to longer-term price moves.
4. The short-term trader will not be in the market for "the big move." It is a valid question to ask whether, in the long run, the short-term trader will make less profit for more effort than the long-term trader. The answer to this question is still not possible to answer since the technological advantages of short-term trading have only been with us for several years. Only time will tell.
5. Short-term trading demands so much time that the individual must have no other form of employment and must make the market his full time occupation.
6. Floor traders and pit brokers still have the time advantage over the public. In the two to three time span that it takes to fill a price order on entry and exit, significant profits might prove to be losses.

Figure 19.1.   Disadvantages of short-term trading

1. Short-term trading requires less margin.
2. In short-term trading you get immediate feedback and you always know the score.
3. Short-term trading has no overnight gaps.
4. With short-term trading there is even less need to know the news.
5. Short-term trading will keep you active in the markets.
6. In short-term trading you will take your losses quickly.
7. Short-term trading gives you less concern. You have less time to think.
8. With short-term trading you have less chart work, and no long-term charts.
9. In short-term trading you are more likely to trade the short side.

Figure 19.2.   Possible advantages of short-term trading

1. A price quotation system or computer with intraday data.
2. A reasonably good trading system.
3. Ability to watch the markets daily on a full time basis.
4. Reasonably low comission rates.
5. Sufficient risk capital.
6. Ability to have price orders executed and reported back to you promptly.
7. Ability to take profits and losses quickly and to keep the proper time perspective in mind at all times.
8. A complete understanding of the markets and, in particular, order placement and types of orders.

Figure 19.3.   Prerequisites for short-term or day trading

20

Some Closing
Words

Now that you have read and, hopefully, studied the concepts and examples I've presented in this book, you should be on the road to positive changes in your investment behavior. In closing, I believe that a few observations, suggestions, and guidelines are in order. I have not spent a great deal of time in organizing these final words since I believe that some of one's best thoughts tend to come at random. When I set out to write this last chapter, I did so from the perspective of an individual who had the opportunity to get answers to questions which could help avoid considerable emotional and financial suffering. I asked myself, "What would I have wanted to know about trading or investment psychology when I was getting started in the markets?" A good majority of my education and self discovery in the markets came to me only through suffering and pain. I had no teacher, no guru, no final authority, and I did not have the good fortune to serve as anyone's apprentice. Futures trading and investing in stocks were not a part of my family tradition and, in fact, my family did not do much to encourage me in that direction since they were not well off financially. Naturally, they felt that a more respectable profession would be medicine or law. The road blocks which were either thrown in my way, or which I threw in my own way, were in retrospect, very beneficial. From each error I found a small piece of the puzzle, and from each success I realized more clearly where the road ahead was taking me. But my story is not as important as are the experiences and observations which shaped my professional growth. If there were lessons to be learned, I learned.

What I hoped to achieve when I started writing this book was not merely a rewrite of *The Investor's Quotient*, but rather a book which picked up where *The Investor's Quotient* left off. Rather than simply "grind out" a book that would rehash old material, I opted to add to *The Investor's Quotient* a fund of knowledge about the psychological aspects of trading and investing. I have done this through eyes which have now matured another four years. I now see things in new perspectives and with greater understanding of process and pragmatics.

I know that my suggestions will not be valuable to all readers; however, I have not attempted to please all. I know this to be an impossible task. Yet, as I stated earlier, if I can motivate readers to set into motion the wheels that foster even the smallest improvement in profits, patience, perception, perseverance, or personal growth, then I feel that my job will have been done.

Perhaps a closing summary of what I have learned in recent years will be beneficial:

1. I have realized that investor and trader psychology are just as important, if not more important, than I have always felt them to be.

2. I know, from more direct experience and observation over the last several years, that the learning process and various stages of learning are of paramount importance in shaping winning or losing behaviors.

3. That behavioral psychology, operant conditioning, behavioral learning theory, and all psychological systems based upon the stimulus–response concept and its variations represent the most logical and effective way of understanding investor behavior.

4. That trading systems are not nearly as important as the public believes them to be.

5. That the strongest and weakest link in the chain of investor success, has always been, and will almost certainly continue to be, the trader.

6. That trader behavior can be changed in positive ways as well as in negative ways.

7. That long-term trading, which was once held on a pedestal as the only type of trading approach for consistent success, is not necessarily as important as I once believed it to be.

8. That computer technology, discount commissions, and more mechanical trading systems can be very helpful in assisting the short-term trader on his or her way to success.

9. That interpersonal relationships are just as important in the markets as they are in one's personal life. Specifically, it is just as important to maintain an effective and clear understanding with your broker as it is to maintain clear lines of communication with your friends, business associates, family, and so on.

10. That faulty learning in the marketplace operates in very subtle ways, particularly when profits are made as a result of, or in spite of, unsystematic, undisciplined, or inappropriate investor behavior.

11. That having a schedule or a mechanical method of trading is one of the most important things a trader can develop.

ABOUT THE FUTURE

As time passes and we discover more efficient, more complicated, and more effective technological aids which should theoretically make the analysis of stock and commodity prices more accurate, there will be a natural tendency to slip farther and farther from the psychological aspects of trading. The illusion that technology and computer science will be the ultimate answer to a person's success in the markets will be further perpetuated by a host of technological developments.

I see the future as even more difficult for those who are not in control of their emotions and attitudes in the markets. I see difficult times ahead for those who have not learned to control and/or change their behaviors. I see less and less emphasis upon the trader's integral role in the investment equation and more and more emphasis upon computers and trading systems. Yet, without the trader, the system cannot function.

I predict that efforts to replace the trader in the investment decision-making process will meet with failure. Investments and speculative trades analyzed by, selected by, and implemented by computers may be an ultimate goal for the "space age" investor. If this can be achieved, then we can eliminate most, if not all, of the negative investor behaviors so common in the markets. The question is, however, "can this indeed become a reality?" Ultimately and at some level, human input is still necessary for technological output. Those who continue to procrastinate changing their behaviors in hopeful anticipation of computer trading, may be waiting "for Godot." It is a poor excuse to put off changes for tomorrow when changes made today could make tomorrow much better.

In closing, I urge all investors, traders, speculators, brokers, in fact, all who are involved in the business of investments and trading, to take an honest look at their results, their behavior, their goals, their consistency, their emotions, and their progress in order to evaluate the best course of action. Were we all to take only one small step toward positive behavior change, we might all take a large step toward greater and more consistent profits.

Bibliography

Altman, L. L. *The Dream of Psychoanalysis*. New York: International Universities Press, 1969.

Beecroft, R. S. *Classical Conditioning*. Goleta, CA: Psychonomic Press, 1966.

Bernstein, J. *The Investor's Quotient*. New York: Wiley, 1980.

Binet, A. and Simon, T. "Le Développement de l'Intelligence Chez les Enfants." *L'Anée Psychologique* **14** (1908): 1–94.

Block, J. *The Challenge of Response Sets*. New York: Appleton-Century-Crofts, 1965.

Boring, E. G. *A History of Experimental Psychology*, 2d ed. New York: Appleton-Century-Crofts, 1950.

Brenner, Charles. *An Elementary Textbook of Psychoanalysis*. Garden City, NY: Anchor Books, 1974.

Broadbent, D. E. *Perception and Communication*. New York: Pergamon Press, 1958.

Caplan, Ruth B. *Psychiatry and the Community in Nineteenth Century America*. New York: Basic Books, 1969.

Capra, Fritjof. *The Tao of Physics*. Boulder, CO: Shabhala Publications, 1975.

Cattell, R. B. *Personality: A Systematic Theoretical and Factual Study*. New York: McGraw-Hill, 1950.

Deese, J. *The Structure of Associations in Language and Thought*. Baltimore: The Johns Hopkins Press, 1965.

Dollard, J. and Miller, N. E. *Personality and Psychotherapy*. New York: McGraw-Hill, 1950.

Eriksen, C. W. "Unconscious Process." In M. R. Jones, ed., *Nebraska Symposium on Motivation*. Lincoln: University of Nebraska Press, 1958, 169–227.

Eriksen, C. W. "Discrimination and Learning Without Awareness, A Methodological Survey and Evaluation." *Psychological Review* **67** (1960): 279–300.

Escalona, S. K. "The Use of Infant Tests for Predictive Purposes." *Bulletin of the Meninger Clinic* **14** (1950): 117–128.

Estes, W. K. "The Statistical Approach to Learning Theory." In S. Koch, ed., *Psychology: A Study of Science*, Vol. 2. New York: McGraw-Hill, 1959.

Ford, D. H. and Urban, H. B. *Systems of Psychotherapy—A Comparative Study*. New York: Wiley, 1965.

Franks, C. M. and Wilson, G. T. *Annual Review of Behavior Therapy: Theory and Practice*. New York: Brunner/Mazel, 1974.

Freud, S. *The Interpretation of Dreams. Collected Works. Vols. 4–5*. London: Hogarth, 1953.

Freud, S. "Three Essays on Sexuality: II-Infantile Sexuality." *Collected Works*. London: Hogarth, 1957.

Gann, W. D. *Truth of the Stock Tape*. Pomeroy, WA: Lambert-Gann, 1923.

Gann, W. D. *How to Make Profits in Commodities*. Pomeroy, WA: Lambert-Gann, 1942.

Gann, W. D. *How to Make Profits in Puts and Calls*. Pomeroy, WA: 1943.

Gann, W. D. *45 Years in Wall Street*. Pomeroy, WA: Lambert-Gann, 1949.

Gesell, A. and Amatruda, C. S. *Developmental Diagnosis*. New York: Harper, 1962.

Gibson, Elanor J. *Principles of Perceptual Learning and Development*. New York: Crofts, 1967.

Gittelson, Bernard. *Biorhythm-A Personal Science*. New York: Arco, 1976.

Goldberg, F. H. and Fiss, H. "Partial Cues and the Phenomenon of Discrimination Without Awareness." *Perceptual Motor Skills* 9 (1959): 243–251.

Hadaday, R. E. *Contrary Opinion*. Pasadena, CA: Market Vane, 1984.

Harlow, H. F. "The Formation of Learning Sets." *Psychological Review* 56: 51–65.

Harlow, H. F. and Woolsey, C. N. (eds.) *Biological and Biochemical Bases of Behavior*. Madison: University of Wisconsin Press, 1958.

Hass, A., Jr. and Jackson, Don D. *The Bulls, Bears and Dr. Freud*. Cleveland, OH: World, 1976.

Henry, William E. *The Analysis of Fantasy*. New York: Wiley, 1956.

Hebb, D. O. *The Organization of Behavior*. New York: Wiley, 1949.

Herb, D. O. "Drives and the C. N. S. (Conceptual Nervous System)." *Psychological Bulletin* 40 (1943): 385–422.

Hull, C. L. "Knowledge and Purpose as Habit Mechanisms." *Psychological Review* 37 (1930): 511–525.

Hull, C. L. *Principles of Behavior*. New York: Appleton-Century-Crofts, 1943.

Hull, C. L. *A Behavior System*. New Haven, CT: Yale University Press, 1952.

Laffal, Julius. *Pathological and Normal Language*. New York: Atherton, 1965.

Lashley, K. S. "Learning: Nervous Mechanisms in Learning." In C. Murchison, ed., *The Foundation of Experimental Psychology*. Worcester, MA: Clark University Press, 1929.

Lashley, K. S. and Wade, M. "The Pavlovian Theory of Generalization." *Psychological Review* **53** (1946): 72–87.

LeFevre, Edwin. *Reminiscences of a Stock Operator*. Larchmont, NY: American Research Council, 1965.

London, Perry. *Behavioral Control*. New York: Meridian, 1977.

McCleary, R. A. and Lazarus, R. S. "Autonomic Discrimination Without Awareness: An Interim Report." *Journal of Personality* **18** (1949): 171–179.

McGeoch, J. A. "Forgetting and the Law of Disuse." *Psychological Review* **39** (1932): 352–70.

Marquis, D. P. "Can Conditioned Responses Be Established in the Newborn Infant?" *Journal of Genetic Psychology* **39** (1931): 479–492.

Marx, M. H. and Hillix, W. A. *Systems and Theories in Psychology*. New York: McGraw-Hill, 1963.

Melton, A. W. *Categories of Human Learning*. New York: Academic, 1964.

Meyer, William J. *Developmental Psychology*. New York: Center for Applied Research in Education, 1964.

Mikvlas, William L. *Concepts in Learning*. Philadelphia: Saunders, 1974.

Mounier, Emmanuel. *The Character of Man*. New York: Harper, 1956.

Mowrer, O. H. "The Psychologist Looks at Language." *American Psychologist* **9** (1954): 660–692.

Mowrer, O. H. *Learning Theory and the Symbolic Process*. New York: Wiley, 1960.

Mowrer, O. H. *Learning Theory and Behavior*. New York: Wiley, 1960.

Murray, H. A. et al. *Explorations in Personality*. New York: Oxford University Press, 1938.

Packard, Vance. *The Hidden Persuaders*. New York: Pocket Books, 1961.

Pavlov, I. P. *Conditioned Reflexes*. Oxford: Clarendon Press, 1927.

Pötzl, O. "The Relationship Between Experimentally Induced Dream Images and Indirect Vision." *Psychological Issues* **2** (3), Monograph 7 (1960): 41–120.

Premack, D. "Reinforcement Theory." In M. R. Jones, ed., *Nebraska Symposium on Motivation: 1965*. Lincoln: University of Nebraska Press, 1965.

Pugh, B. *The Science and Secrets of Wheat Trading*. Pomeroy, WA: Lambert-Gann, 1978; orig. 1933.

Pugh, B. *A Better Way to Make Money*. Pomeroy, WA: Lambert-Gann, 1948.

Secord, P. F. and Backman, Carl W. *Social Psychology*. New York: McGraw-Hill, 1964.

Selye, H. *The Physiology and Pathology of Exposure to Stress*. Montreal: Acta, 1950.

Skinner, B. F. "On the Conditions of Elicitation of Certain Eating Reflexes." *Proceedings of the National Academy of Sciences* **16** (1930): 433–438.

Skinner, B. F. "The Concept of the Reflex in the Description of Behavior." *Journal of General Psychology* **5** (1931): 427–58. Reprinted in B. F. Skinner. *Cumulative*

Record. New York: Appleton-Century-Crofts, 1959, pp. 319–46.

Skinner, B. F. "On the Rate of Formation of a Conditioned Reflex," *Journal of General Psychology*, **7** (1932): 274–286. Reprinted in A. C. Cazania, ed., *Contemporary Research in Operant Behavior.* Glenview, IL: Scott, Foresman, 1968, pp. 48–52.

Skinner, B. F. "The Behavior of Organisms: An Experimental Psychology," **38** (1948): 168–72. Reprinted in A. C. Catania, ed., *Contemporary Research in Operant Behavior.* Glenview, IL: Scott, Foresman, 1968, pp. 62–64.

Skinner, B. F. *Walden Two.* New York: Macmillan, 1948.

Skinner, B. F. "Are Theories of Learning Necessary?" *Psychological Review* **57** (1950). Reprinted in A. C. Catania, ed., *Contemporary Research in Operant Behavior.* Glenview, IL: Scott, Foresman, 1968, pp. 4–21.

Skinner, B. F. *Science and Human Behavior.* New York: Macmillan, 1953.

Skinner, B. F. *Verbal Behavior.* New York: Appleton-Century-Crofts, 1957.

Spence, K. W. "The Role of Secondary Reinforcement in Delayed-Reward Learning." *Psychological Review* **54** (1947): 1–8.

Thorndike, E. L. *Animal Intelligence.* New York: Macmillan, 1911.

Thorndike, E. L. "The Psychology of Learning," in *Educational Psychology*, Vol. II. New York: Teacher's College, Columbia University, 1913.

Thorndike, E. L. *The Fundamentals of Learning.* New York: Teacher's College, Columbia University, 1932.

Thurstone, L. L. *Personality Schedule.* Chicago: University of Chicago Press, 1929.

Tolman, E. C. "A Behavioristic Account of the Emotions." *Psychological Review*, **30** (1923): 217–227.

Tolman, E. C. *Purposive Behavior in Animals and Men.* New York: Appleton-Century-Crofts, 1932.

Ullman, L. P. and Krasner, L. (eds.) *Case Studies in Behavior Modification.* New York: Holt, Rinehart & Winston, 1965.

Watson, J. B. "Psychology as the Behaviorist Sees It." *Psychological Review* **20** (1913): 158–177.

Watson, J. B. *Psychology from the Standpoint of a Behaviorist.* Philadelphia: Lippincott, 1919.

Watson, J. B. "A Schematic Outline of the Emotions." *Psychological Review* **26** (1919): 165–96.

Watson, J. B. *Behaviorism.* New York: Norton, 1924.

Watts, A. W. *The Book on the Taboo Against Knowing Who You Are.* New York: Vintage, 1972.

Watzlawick, Paul, et al. *Pragmatics of Human Communication.* New York: Norton, 1967.

Wiener, M. and Schiller, P. H. "Subliminal Perception or Perception of Partial Cues." *Journal of Abnormal Social Psychology* **61** (1960): 124–137.

Wolman, Benjamin (ed.) *Handbook of General Psychology.* Englewood Cliffs, NJ: Prentice-Hall, 1973.

Index